Collecting

Comic Character
CLOCKS
and
WATCHES

By Howard S. Brenner

BOOKS AMERICANA
INC

ISBN 0-89689-062-7

DEDICATION

For my father

TABLE OF CONTENTS

FOREWORD

As a child, I remember waiting in anticipation for my favorite television show, constantly asking my father ''Is it time yet?'' Apparently, this became somewhat of an annoyance, since on my seventh birthday I was given my first timepiece – a genuine Davy Crocket wristwatch, complete with a powder horn! Now, I could act out my childhood fantasies of exploring the ''new frontier'' and still be able to check my new watch to be home in time for dinner.

Almost everyone can relate to a similar experience of receiving his first timepiece. In fact, the advertising genuises of childrens' playthings immediately noticed this and went on to produce some of the most intricately detailed and graphically beautiful timepieces of popular comic strip, radio and television personalities. If they had realized then that such an inexpensive child's item would now command hundreds of dollars, I'm sure they would have packed away cases of them for their retirement.

Fortunately for us, no one has done this; therefore, there is still that tintillating thrill of searching for a new acquisition to add to our collections.

Comic character timepieces have personalties all their own, from the cherub-faced, ever-popular Mickey Mouse pocket watch to the animated six-gun of the Gene Autry wristwatch.

As a professional toy dealer for the past fifteen years, I've seen the popularity of collecting these ticking timepieces grow tremendously. The need for a comprehensive price guide has never been greater.

I know of no one who is better equipped to accomplish this task than Howard Brenner. He knows his subject well. This remarkable photographic reference will serve both beginning and advanced collectors with extensive coverage of the entire comic timepiece market. I know you will find it a valuable addition to your library.

Happy Collecting!
Mark Karpinski

ACKNOWLEDGEMENTS

A great many people contributed to the preparation of this book.

First, and foremost, very special thanks to Ken Pamatat of Creative Images for his superb photography and dedication to excellence.

For supplying photos and/or information, many thanks to Jim Allen, Don Brooks, Dan Crawley, Stu Foreman, Ted Hake, Bill Koroch, Walt Pawtulski, Lee Sierens, Cosmo Sorice and Ron Vermette.

My heartfelt thanks to Bob Lesser for graciously allowing us to use selected photos from his collection.

Special gratitude to Mark Karpinski for his friendship, patience and guidance.

Very special gratitude to Books Americana publisher Dan Alexander for his enthusiasm and encouragement.

And finally, ultimate gratitude to my wife Sandra for her love, support and continued understanding.

PREFACE

One of the most frustrating aspects of collecting comic character timepieces has been the lack of information. With little or no reference materials available, collectors have had to learn as they acquire – virtually collecting ''in the dark.''

This has led to wide price variations (usually on the high side) as well as mis-identification by well-meaning but uninformed dealers and collectors.

This book is my attempt to rectify that. Over two years in planning and research, this is the result: the first comprehensive look at the entire spectrum of comic character timepieces - a guide which will enable you to recognize, identify and evaluate all currently known pieces.

Please note that I make no claim this book is all-inclusive. As with any first effort, it is inevitable that errors will occur and omissions will be made. I trust that both have been kept to a minimum.

Because the publisher plans to issue an updated version of this book in the future, I would like to hear from others who may have information or items not included here. I would especially like to hear from you if you worked for any of the comic character timepiece manufacturers during the 1930s, 1940s or 1950s.

In addition, I am desirous of acquiring printed materials such as catalogues issued by manufacturers, distributors, wholesalers, jobbers and retailers, point-of-purchase displays, promotional literature, newspaper and magazine ads, store displays, price sheets, etc.

I also welcome your suggestions, comments and constructive criticism. Please write to me at 106 Woodgate Terrace, Rochester, New York 14625.

One final note: Because first editions of many price guides are so eagerly awaited, they tend to be treated as gospel. I offer this book not as a commandment or holy writ, but rather as a reference work deriving its authority from the care, diligence and completeness with which its facts were researched, compiled and analyzed. Its primary purpose is to be an accurate, reliable and useful reference source, enabling you to deal knowledgeably and realistically in the marketplace.

I hope you will find the book to be both rewarding and informative.

Howard S. Brenner
September 1986

INTRODUCTION

There's no doubt about it – we're a nation of savers and collectors. From arrowheads, barbed wire and coins to stamps, typewriters and valentines, people are collecting like never before.

Nowhere is this better reflected than in the growing popularity of specialized collectible shows for such items as toys, dolls, comic books, baseball cards and the like. These shows have sharply focused interest and attention on current collecting trends and prices.

One popular area of growing interest is the field of comic character timepieces – those inexpensive childrens' novelty watches and clocks produced during the 1930s, 1940s and 1950s. Once dismissed as junk, they are today proving to be highly collectible and valuable.

One reason is their universal appeal. Many children were given a novelty timepiece when they first learned to tell time. Seeing that item again today often brings back a flood of happy childhood memories – along with the desire to once again own the piece.

However, the supply is extremely limited due to the very nature of the item itself. Because these were novelty watches, often produced to capitalize on the sudden popularity of a character or fad, production runs were very short.

Remember, too, that these timepieces were for children to use (and abuse) and enjoy. Made to sell for just a few dollars, these ''pin lever'' movements could be produced inexpensively. Unfortunately, they could not easily be repaired. Since the cost of fixing one often would exceed the original cost, most were simply thrown away when they failed. Thus, they are difficult to find today in any condition.

Unfortunately, too, most parents threw away the colorfully decorated boxes the clocks and watches came in – making the boxes even rarer than the timepieces they accompanied. When one turns up mint in the box, usually from an old jewelry or department store, prices can be very high.

Another factor limiting today's supply is that relative to the economy of the 1930s and early 1940s, these timepieces were rather expensive. Back then, breakfast cereal was 9¢ a box, hamburger was 10¢ a pound, and a ready-made suit could be bought for just $10! The average take-home wage was $12 per week.

Priced at $2.98, a child's watch represented an enormous chunk of the weekly budget. It's not surprising that many children did not receive these timepieces as birthday or Christmas presents during the dark days of the Depression.

Thus, with the supply limited, but with demand increasing, comic character timepieces are slowly ascending the ladder of collectible popularity. Perhaps its because more than most collectibles, comic character timepieces allow us to tangibly re-capture our childhood memories – to plug-in to the past. By acquiring one of these delightful timepieces, a piece of history actually comes alive.

Yes, the clocks and watches that thrilled us as children now reach out to us as adults! Never was the axiom more true than today: one man's junk is another man's joy.

HOW TO USE THIS BOOK

All items are listed alphabetically using the first name of the character. For example, Capt. Marvel is under ''C'', Dick Tracy is under ''D'', Orphan Annie is under ''O'' and so on. Within listings for the same character, clocks are listed first, followed by pocket watches and wristwatches.

Because we have endeavored to make this book as complete and comprehensive as possible, we have listed and shown similar items which exhibit variations in their boxes, cases or styles. For example, the Hopalong Cassidy wristwatch came with both plastic and metal cases, in two different sizes and in two different boxes!

Above the photo of each timepiece is the date it was first produced and the name of its manufacturer. Any relevant information is then presented, although many photos are self-explanatory and there is no accompanying text.

Finally, pricing is provided for each item in four different categories – good, very good/fine, excellent and mint in box. Be sure to read the description of each category in the following section.

CONDITION

Condition is crucial to value, yet comic character timepiece collectors have had no set of standards to guide them. Because grading is a subjective art at best, it is important to establish a grading system that is both precise and easy to use, without regard for sentimentality. That first Mickey Mouse pocket watch you ever owned may still be in excellent condition to your own eyes, but to an unbiased, critical collector, it may actually rate only very good.

In addition, many transactions are now occurring by phone or mail. Failure to have a "meeting of the minds" beforehand about the exact condition of the item can often lead to disappointment or anger.

Therefore, we propose to establish a single set of standards by which to accurately grade all comic character timepieces. Here are the guidelines we followed:

First, and most important, the terms used are **not** relative to age – they are absolute. Age is neither a determining nor a contributing factor. Mint means "brand new, like the day it came out of the factory," with no qualifications.

For example, a boxed watch which has been left out in the sun and now exhibits fading should not be called "mint." Its proper description is "watch (mint), box (faded)."

Similarly, a boxed watch that has been stored in a damp basement and now exhibits rust should not be called "mint." Its proper description is "watch (never used, exhibits rust), box (mint)."

Over and over, collectors hear the phrase "It's in nice shape considering its age." To repeat: Age has no bearing on the determination of condition.

Second, we are assuming for the mint in box category that the item is indeed in its proper, original box. Unfortunately, we have recently noticed the disturbing trend of items in mint condition (some even with original price tags) turning up in "generic" boxes, the boxes used for the standard line. These are usually plain boxes with the manufacturer's name on it. For comic character timepieces, these boxes are not correct!

To date, after examining hundreds of clocks and watches, the author has verified only two exceptions to this rule – the 1946 Kelton Mickey Mouse wristwatch and the 1947 Deluxe series of Disney wristwatches. Otherwise, all other comic character timepieces came in colorfully printed boxes. After all, they were childrens' items – meant to appeal to youngsters – and the packaging was graphically meant to catch a child's attention.

If someone tries to sell you a comic character timepiece in a "generic" box – be wary!

With these criteria in mind, here are our grading standards. We hope everyone will find them useful:

MINT IN BOX: Mint in its original box. Absolutely brand-new and perfect in every way. Looks just as nice as the day it was made. Must be completely original. Box has no fading, stains, tears, rips, etc. May or may not have original price tag. Watch has never been worn, clock has never been used. Box must have all inserts.

EXCELLENT: Almost perfect. Any defects are minor in nature. Wristwatch has original straps which may show very slight wear. Crystal is free of scratches, dial is bright and clean. For clocks and pocket watches, dial and cases are bright and clean, crystal is blemish-free. Does not show surface imperfections such as dents, rust, scratches, nicks, chips, etc.

VERY GOOD/FINE: Obviously used. A wider ranging category. Wristwatch still has original straps, but has obviously been worn. Crystal may have some scratches, dial may be a bit faded or show some wear. For clocks and pocket watches, dial, case and crystal may show signs of wear. Small nicks, scratches and dents may be present.

GOOD: Heavily used. Wristwatch may or may not have original strap. Shows considerable wear and tear. Crystal has many scratches or may be entirely missing. Dial faded, darkened or soiled. May also be dented or rusted. Items in this condition should be acquired only by "diehard" collectors who are willing to settle for any example of a very rare or difficult to obtain item.

Try to buy your timepieces in the best possible condition. As with other collectibles, top quality brings top prices and sells quickly. A good rule of thumb to remember is: It's always best to own an item that others desire to buy, rather than an item you have to sell.

Unfortunately, many new collectors, caught-up in the enthusiasm of "the hunt," disregard this rule. They buy everything in sight, regardless of condition, because it's cheap, thinking that someday, when a better example surfaces, they'll "trade-up." Unless you are extremely wealthy and can afford to have large sums of money tied up in your hobby, this approach is foolhardy.

Since most advanced collectors only want items in the best condition, you will have trouble selling your poorer quality items. Your objective should be to buy the item once – in the very best condition – mint in box, if possible.

Be especially alert for reproductions and outright fakes! As the interest has grown and prices have risen, unscrupulous operators have started faking many items. Most widely counterfeited is the Ingersoll Mickey Mouse pocket watch, although fake Buck Rogers and Betty Boop pocket watches have also been spotted. Some of these are so well made that they are difficult to tell from the originals. Unsuspecting or naive collectors can easily be fooled. Although dealing with reputable dealers and collectors will minimize your chances of getting burned, your best defense is a good offense – that is, learn all you can about comic character timepieces!

PRICING

This is the section most people will probably consult first and is probably the reason many of you purchased this book — you want to learn how much your comic character timepiece is worth. This is how we determined values for every item:

First, we consulted with leading dealers, major auction houses and knowledgeable private collectors. Then, we attended many specialized toy and collectible shows, clock and watch conventions, as well as antique shows and specialty auctions. Plus, we visited numerous dealer shops and flea markets. Finally, from these wide and diverse sources, we distilled pertinent price trends about each item to arrive at our final values.

The prices listed are retail selling prices — what you'd expect to pay a knowledgeable collector or dealer to obtain the item in the condition listed. We have tried to be as fair and accurate as possible. However, these prices are only a guide, giving you an approximate indication of value. No one is bound by them. Keep in mind, also, that these prices are not like those for gold and silver, which you can follow on a daily basis in your newspaper. There is no ''National Price Fixing'' for comic character timepieces!

At any given moment, it is possible that identical items in two different locations may change hands at two different prices. The reasons are many: geographic location, buyer's enthusiasm, dealer's knowledge, dealer's inventory, economic conditions, current fads or trends, even the season!

The best way to be certain of getting the best deal is to become a knowledgeable collector yourself. Learn all you can. First, of course, read this book. Then, attend toy shows, become friendly with dealers and collectors in your area and subscribe to leading antique newspapers and toy magazines. Arm yourself with as much information as possible. Experience and knowledge are your best weapons!

Supply and Demand

Like any other commodity, comic character timepieces are subject to the laws of supply and demand. The rarest item in the world is worth nothing if there is no demand for it. Conversely, relatively common items may command high prices because of steady demand.

To vividly illustrate how this works in the comic character timepiece market, let's take two items: the 1946 Kelton Mickey Mouse wristwatch and the 1933 Ingersoll Mickey Mouse pocket watch.

The Kelton was the first Mickey Mouse wristwatch produced after the war. Due to material shortages, few were produced. Today it is extremely scarce. However, because the number of collectors who desire to own it is so small, its value is relatively low.

The Ingersoll pocket watch, on the other hand, is fairly common. Millions were produced. It is far easier to find than the Kelton. However, because the number of collectors who desire to own it is extremely large, its value is relatively high.

Don't be fooled then, if you discover an obscure item, into thinking that you have found gold. Yes, it may be rare — it may even be the only one of its kind ever found. But — if there is little or no demand for it, you will receive only a low price — truly reflecting the indisputable laws of supply and demand.

Two other closely related terms to keep in mind are ''rarity'' and ''desirability.'' While they may seem similar, there is a world of difference. An item is ''rare'' because few examples of it are known to exist. An item is ''desirable'' because large numbers of collectors wish to own it. As with the illustration of the Kelton watch, just because an item is rare does not mean it is desirable.

Selling Your Timepieces

The time may come when you wish to sell some or all of your collection. There are several methods to consider.

The quickest and most efficient way is to sell your collection as a lot directly to a dealer. However, do not expect him to pay you the prices in this book. Remember, these are retail selling prices. A dealer must make a profit to stay in business, and he has related expenses. He will want to pay you a wholesale price, somewhere between 50% to 70% of retail.

If time is not of the essence, and you wish to obtain closer to market value for your collection, there are two other methods. One is to sell to private collectors. Although they may be willing to pay closer to book value, they may already own many of the more common items you have and may only want to "cherry pick" your rarest or most desirable items, still leaving you the problem of where to dispose of the remainder.

The other method is to put together a sales list of the items you have and advertise them in antique newspapers and specialized collector magazines to get the widest exposure possible. Be sure to be accurate in describing the condition of your items. A drawback to this method is that there are expenses involved – for printing, postage and advertising – that will decrease your profit. Also, this can be time consuming if you have a large number of items to sell.

Frequently Asked Questions

Q. Are comic character timepieces a good investment?

A. While it is true that values for most comic character timepieces have risen steadily over the years, past performance is no guarantee of the future. The vast majority of collectors buy them because of the enjoyment they provide, rather than looking for potential investment gains. Investing for profit or a "quick killing" is usually not a good idea. Unless you have expert knowledge about the field, you can easily be taken advantage of. More than one collector has been sold an "original" Mickey Mouse wristwatch and paid accordingly, only to later discover that the watch was the 1947 model, worth considerably less than what they paid. The best way to "invest" in a hobby is to learn all you can about it, buy wisely, and profit from the enjoyment your collection gives you.

Q. I heard that in a mail order auction, a Mickey Mouse pocket watch sold for $500, yet you list it at $275. Why the difference?

A. The popularity of mail order auctions has given people in remote areas of the country the chance to bid on and acquire items they might not otherwise be able to obtain. Being located far from local or regional toy shows, these people are not able to keep up with current price trends. Thus, they may be willing to pay in excess of current market value to obtain particular items.

Another reason could be "auction fever." Many times participants get so caught up in the fevered pitch of the bidding that prices realized are higher than actual market value.

Also, there may be one bidder who has been looking for that one particular item for a long time, and is now willing to pay nearly anything to acquire it.

Remember that prices in this book are only a guide. Unusual circumstances may dictate a higher price. What you ultimately pay will be determined by your intensity to acquire the item and by the value it has to you.

Q. At toy and antique shows lately, I've been noticing items for sale at prices higher than you indicate. Why is this?

A. You may very well find an item you'd like to own priced somewhat higher than we've indicated in this book. Say, for example, we value the item at $150 and the dealer price is $175. Most dealers are willing to bargain and have left some room in their asking price for this. Offer the dealer $150. It is likely that he will either accept your offer or make you a counteroffer. Don't be afraid to haggle for a better price. It is the rare dealer whose original asking price is set in stone.

It is also entirely possible that if you are seeing **consistently** higher (30% or more) prices, a trend of rising prices has begun. Although we have attempted to make this book as current as possible, by the time you read it this pricing information could be out-of-date due to market dynamics.

Prices can rise or fall due to outside factors. A small warehouse or jewelry store find – as happened several years ago with the 1947 and 1950 Mickey Mouse wristwatches – may hit the market, temporarily depressing prices.

Conversely, favorable publicity about a particular character or item may spark a price rise. Even the publication of this book and its accompanying publicity may cause prices to rise if a new wave of collectors hits the market.

We can't stress this point enough: these prices are only a guide. They are not an attempt to set retail prices, nor are they prices that anyone is bound by.

Q. Why do you strongly advise collectors to try to obtain all their items mint in box?

A. Collecting timepieces without boxes is like whistling at a pretty girl in the dark – you miss half the fun. For example, between 1950 and 1958, US Time produced the same Mickey Mouse wristwatch. If you collect just the watch, you have one item to show for that eight year span. If, however, you collect the boxes as well, you have five different variations to collect and display.

In addition, because many watches are being reproduced and faked, buying mint in box completely eliminates your chances of being taken. Crooks can easily fake an inexpensive watch, but to duplicate the colorful boxes requires expensive printing equipment and extensive printing knowledge, making it highly unlikely that a box could be faked.

Of course, for some items, mainly pocket watches and clocks, the boxes are extremely scarce and difficult to obtain. A good rule to follow is: if it's pictured in this book with its original box, your objective should be to obtain it in the same condition.

Q. Should the timepiece I buy be working?

A. Whether or not a timepiece works is of little concern to most collectors. Since the majority of timepieces don't have second hands, there is no way to visually tell if one is working or not. Collectors realize that the inexpensive movements tended to wear out quickly and that any lubrication originally used has long since dried out. Many collectors will wind a timepiece, just to hear a few reassuring ticks and to be sure the movement is complete, but for the most part whether or not a timepiece works will have little effect on prices. Many of these timepieces are so rare that collectors would be thrilled just to find one – working or not!

A SHORT HISTORY OF COMIC CHARACTER TIMEPIECES

Mention the words "comic character timepiece" to someone and he will invariably reply "Oh, you mean a Mickey Mouse watch!" For it was indeed Mickey Mouse – or rather his creator Walt Disney – who started the entire "comic character timepiece" industry in 1933 when the Ingersoll-Waterbury Company of Waterbury, Connecticut was granted a license to produce a complete line of Mickey Mouse timepieces: a wristwatch which sold for $3.75, and a pocket watch, electric clock and a wind-up clock which retailed for $1.50 each.

The line proved so successful that Ingersoll, which earlier had been in receivership and was again nearly bankrupt, was literally saved by Mickey Mouse! When production began in June of 1933, the financially shaky company employed just 300 people. After only eight weeks of production, demand was so great that an additional 2700 employees had to be hired.

By the end of the year, 900,000 clocks and watches had come off the assembly line. Demand was incredible! In New York City, Macy's Department Store reportedly sold as many as 11,000 watches in a single day!

By March of 1935, the company was Disney's biggest licensee, and on June 1, 1935, it announced that over 2½ million wristwatches had been sold.

Ingersoll's financial good fortune did not go unnoticed by the competition. Although it held an exclusive license for all Disney characters, there were plenty of others available, and soon, virtually all of them peered out from their very own timepieces.

Buck Rogers and Betty Boop came to us courtesy of Ingraham, while New Haven offered Popeye, Superman, the Lone Ranger, Dick Tracy, Orphan Annie and Smitty. The Wilane Watch Company galloped in with Gene Autry and Ingersoll, which had started the whole fad, added The Three Little Pigs, Tom Mix and Donald Duck to its line.

The new industry's popularity continued to grow until it was abruptly halted by the outbreak of World War Two. Deemed "non-essential" by the government, production immediately ceased "for the duration" as factories were converted to wartime use. The Ingersoll plant, for example, was re-tooled to produce military fuses for the armed forces.

By 1946, with wartime shortages over, production could be resumed. However, Americans were now more concered with resuming normal post-war lives and rebuilding war-torn families. They had little time to spend on frivolous things, and comic character timepieces never regained their pre-war popularity.

Appearing for the first time on post-war comic watches were such timely favorites as Capt. Marvel, Mary Marvel, Roy Rogers, Dale Evans, Bugs Bunny, Joe Palooka, Hopalong Cassidy, Howdy Doody and Woody Woodpecker.

Ingersoll (now operating as US Time) continued to produce its reliable Mickey Mouse clocks and watches, and by 1948 had manufactured 5,000,000 watches. Nine years later, in 1957, the 25,000,00th watch rolled off the production line and was personally presented to Walt Disney.

By now, however, it was becoming apparent that even Mickey Mouse was running out of steam as sales of all comic timepieces continued to sag. The handwriting was on the wall – the fad of character watches had run its course. A year later, 1958, production of all comic watches ceased.

Ten years later, a nostalgia boom swept the country, bringing with it a renewed interest in Mickey Mouse watches. Timex (formerly US Time) decided to cautiously test the marketing waters once again. To commemorate Mickey's 40th Birthday, three watches were produced: a $12.95 wind-up Mickey, a $12.95 wind-up Minnie, and a $19.95 electric Mickey. The total production, meant to last a year, was nibbled away in less than a month.

For some reason, however, Timex was not interested in continuing comic watch production, and ended its contract with Disney. One of the longest and most lucrative contracts in the history of merchandising had come to an end.

From 1969 to 1971, no Mickey watches were made. Then, in 1972, Helbros signed on to produce a line of Mickey, Minnie and Goofy watches. Unfortunately, in a disastrous marketing decision, they made a 17-jewel, lithographed dial watch retailing for $19.95. Although they were beautifully designed and made, the ''sticker shock'' price doomed retail sales and the line was discontinued after a short run. However, the unusual backwards Goofy watch (see listing for a complete description) has attained a highly collectible status.

The following year, Bradley took over production. By substituting cheaper dials and movements, they were able to reduce prices and increase sales. In recent years they have issued special commemorative watches for Disneyland's 25th and 30th Birthdays, the Opening of Epcot Center, Mickey Mouse's 50th Birthday, Donald Duck's 50th Birthday, and the 50th Anniversary of the Mickey Mouse watch.

With few exceptions, however, the regular production has been unimaginative and undistinguished. Worse, the line has been poorly distributed, making it hard to find. By the end of 1985, Bradley had relinquished its license and stopped making Disney watches.

In 1986, Lorus became the newest member of the Disney family and in June issued its initial line of five quartz watches retailing for $29.95. Will these watches be future collectibles? Only time will tell.

ALICE IN WONDERLAND
1950 – U. S. TIME

Beautifully decorated box features scenes from the film. Plastic watch is common. Box is quite rare.
Good – $10; Very Good/Fine – $30; Mint – $50; Mint in Box – $200

ALICE IN WONDERLAND
1958 – TIMEX

On later versions, watch scene is replaced by the word "Alice".
Good – $8; Very Good/Fine – $24; Mint – $40; Mint in Box – $125

BABE RUTH
1949 – EXACTA TIME

Watch is fairly common. Expansion band is original and correct. Box and baseball are extremely rare.
Good – $30; Very Good/Fine – $90; Mint – $150; Mint in Box – $300

BAMBI
1964 – BAYARD

One of a series of Disney clocks made in France. Limited U.S. distribution. Animated: Butterfly moves back and forth.
Good – $15; Very Good/Fine – $45; Mint – $75; Mint in Box – $100

BAMBI
1949 – INGERSOLL (U.S. TIME)

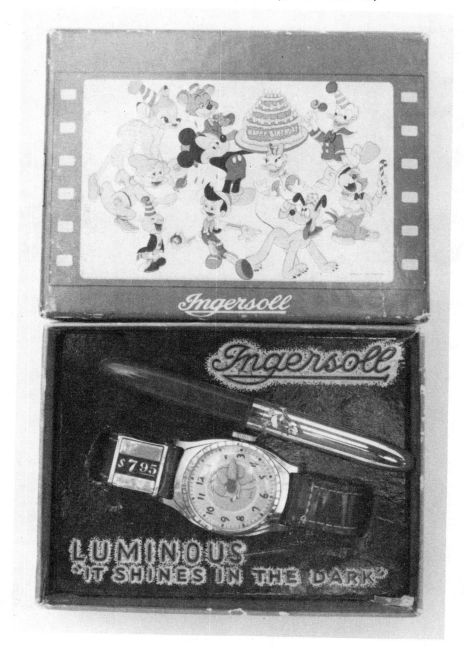

One of the ten "Birthday Series" watches produced to celebrate Mickey Mouse's 20th Birthday.
Good – $25; Very Good/Fine – $75; Mint – $125; Mint in Box – $250

BATMAN
1978 – TIMEX

Produced in Canada, received limited U.S. distribution.

Good – $7; Very Good/Fine – $21; Mint – $35; Mint in Box – $50

BETTY BOOP
1934 – INGRAHAM

Failed to originally catch on since only boys carried pocket watches, and they preferred Buck Rogers or Mickey Mouse. Few survive today. Ultra rare – less than ten known to exist. Must have die-debossed back to be completely original.

Good – $70; Very Good/Fine – $210; Mint – $350; Mint in Box – $500

BUCK ROGERS
1935 – INGRAHAM

Fairly common. Beware of reproductions. Must have ''lightning bolt'' hands and ''one-eyed monster'' on reverse.

Good – $70; Very Good/Fine – $210; Mint – $350; Mint in Box – $550

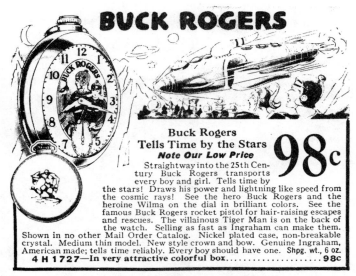

1935 Sears Advertisement

BUGS BUNNY
1951 – INGRAHAM

Animated "time-telling dial" features Bugs eating his carrot, which moves up and down.

Good – $30; Very Good/Fine – $90; Mint – $150; Mint in Box – $225

BUGS BUNNY
1951 – WARNER BROS.

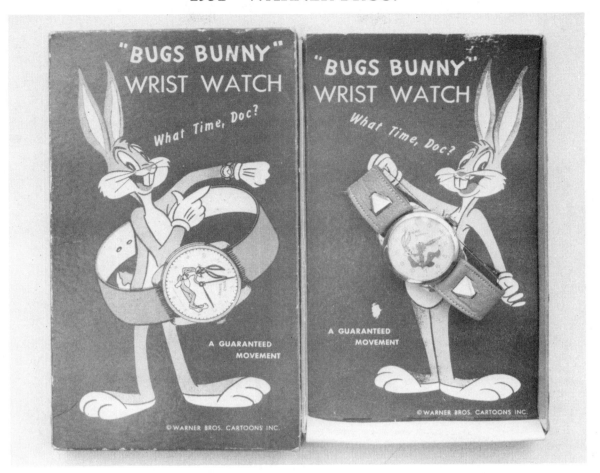

Hard to find today since it was ''Imported exclusively for the Rexall Drug Co.'' and only sold in **Rexall Drug** Stores.

Good – $25; Very Good/Fine – $75; Mint – $125; Mint in Box – **$200**

BUZZ COREY'S SPACE PATROL
1951 – U.S. TIME

Common watch betrays uncommon and extremely rare packaging. Box alone has sold for $300 and up.
Good – $17; Very Good/Fine – $51; Mint – $85; Mint in Box – $350

CAPT. LIBERTY
1951 – LIBERTY WATCH CO.

Underside of box reads: "The Capt. Liberty Spaceman Watch is a real wristwatch. It is a rugged, dependable timekeeper with a jewelled, anti-magnetic movement for greater accuracy. The handsome Capt. Liberty space dial tells universal time and glows in the dark. This gift package has been designed to make a perfect Space Observation Post and contains universally interesting space information." Extremely unusual and rare.

Good –$20; Very Good/Fine – $60; Mint – $100; Mint in Box – $250

CAPT. MARVEL (DELUXE)
1948 – FAWCETT

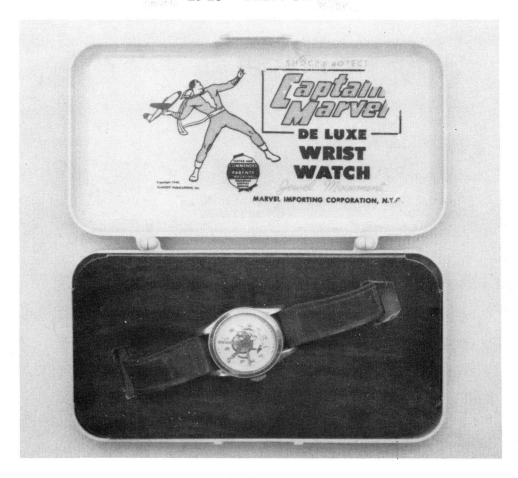

Plastic box with small size, one-jewel movement watch, came with colorful vinylite band. This packaging style is uncommon, since the watch originally sold for $1 more than the non-jewel watch.

Good – $20; Very Good/Fine – $60; Mint – $100; Mint in Box – $225

CAPT. MARVEL
1948 – FAWCETT

Larger size than the deluxe. Fairly common and easy to find. Vinylite bands come in red, green and blue.
Good – $20; Very Good/Fine – $60; Mint – $100; Mint in Box – $200

CHARLIE McCARTHY
1938 – GILBERT

Animated. Charlie's mouth opens and closes. Scarce.

Good –$75; Very Good/Fine – $225; Mint – $375; Mint in Box – $500

CINDERELLA
1950 – U.S. TIME

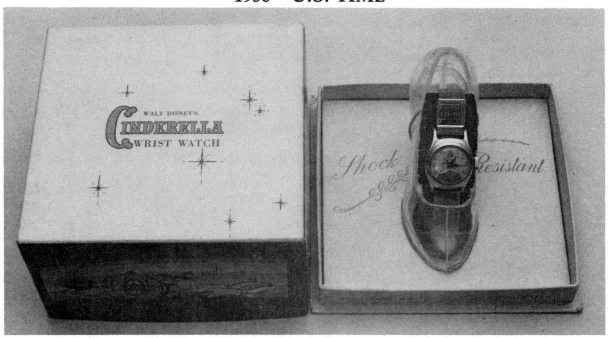

Colorfully decorated "Slipper Box" features scenes from the film. Metal watch is very common. Packaging is rare. Also came in a round box.

Good – $10; Very Good/Fine – $30; Mint – $50; Mint in Box – $225

CINDERELLA
1956 – TIMEX

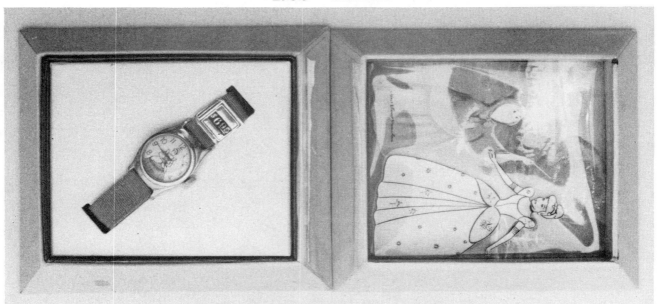

Same metal watch as previous listing. Inside box top features scene from the movie on a colorful plastic sheet. Unusual and uncommon.

Good – $10; Very Good/Fine – $30; Mint – $50; Mint in Box – $200

CINDERELLA
1958 – TIMEX

Statue on left is porcelain, statue on right is plastic.

Good – $10; Very Good/Fine – $30; Mint – $50; Mint in Box – $125

DALE EVANS

1951 – INGRAHAM

Unusual "pop-up" display box. Same watch available with either expansion band or western-look leather band.
Good – $10; Very Good/Fine – $30; Mint – $50; Mint in Box – $150

DAN DARE
1953 – INGERSOLL LTD.

Only "double animation" pocket watch ever found. Dan's arm goes up and down while the rocket ship second-hand below him revolves. Dan Dare was a popular English comic strip hero – the equivalent of our Buck Rogers.
Good – $55; Very Good/Fine – $165; Mint – $275; Mint in Box – $325

DAVY CROCKETT
1954 – HADDON

Animated electric clock. The horse bucks poor Davy up and down while the bear attacks. Few were sold due to its unbelievable price – $40! Very rare.

Good – $35; Very Good/Fine – $105; Mint – $175; Mint in Box – $225

DAVY CROCKETT
1954 – U.S. TIME

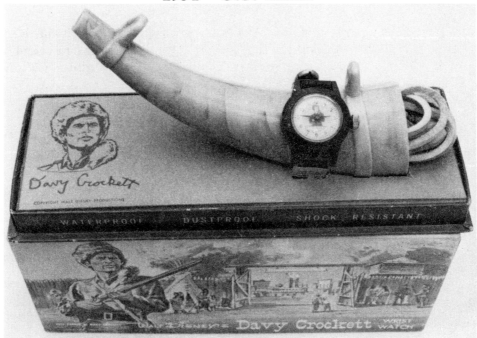

Highly desired by western collectors.   Good – $10; Very Good/Fine – $30; Mint – $50; Mint in Box – $150

DAVY CROCKETT
1955 – MANUFACTURER UNKNOWN

Pendulette clock.

Good – $15; Very Good/Fine – $45; Mint – $75; Mint in Box – $125

DAVY CROCKETT
1956 – BRADLEY

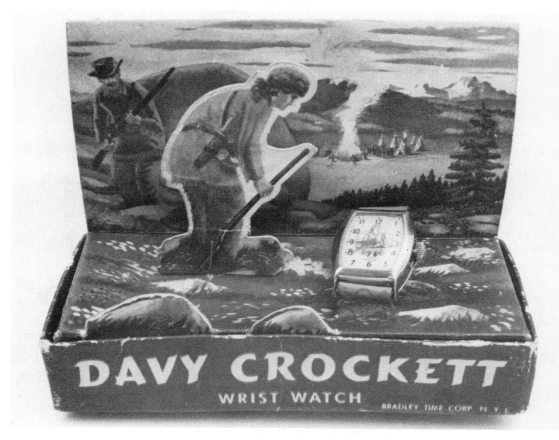

"3-D" pop-up box features Davy in front of a western scene. Watch is fairly common. Unique box is rare.
Good – $13; Very Good/Fine – $39; Mint – $65; Mint in Box – $175

DICK TRACY

1948 – NEW HAVEN

Watch also came in a square case.

Good – $20; Very Good/Fine – $60;
Mint – $100; Mint in Box – $225

DICK TRACY

1951 – NEW HAVEN

Animated: Dick's pistol moves back and forth.

Good – $30; Very Good/Fine – $90;
Mint – $150; Mint in Box – $200

DIZZY DEAN
1935 – NEW HAVEN

Highly desired by baseball collectors.

Good – $30; Very Good/Fine – $90; Mint – $150; Mint in Box – $200

DIZZY DEAN
1935 – EVERBRITE WATCH CO.

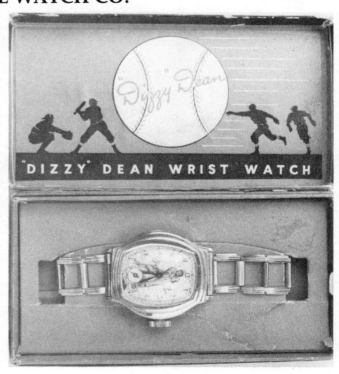

Highly desired by baseball collectors.

Good –$30; Very Good/Fine – $90;
Mint – $150; Mint in Box – $250

DONALD DUCK
1950 – GLEN CLOCK

Made in Scotland. Animated: Donald's head moves back and forth in front of colorful scene. Rare.
Good – $40; Very Good/Fine – $120; Mint – $200; Mint in Box – $250

DONALD DUCK
1964 – BAYARD

One of a series of Disney clocks made in France. Limited distribution in U.S. Animated: Donald's head moves back and forth.

Good –$15; Very Good/Fine – $45; Mint – $75; Mint in Box – $100

DONALD DUCK

1939 – INGERSOLL

Many feature a decal of Mickey on the back. Originally sold poorly, so they are scarce today.

Good – $80; Very Good/Fine – $240; Mint – $400; Mint in Box – $550

DONALD DUCK
1936 – INGERSOLL

Features a Mickey Mouse second hand and band. Originally sold poorly, so Mickey was put on to help. Rare.
Good – $25; Very Good/Fine – $75; Mint – $125; Mint in Box – $250

DONALD DUCK
1947 – U.S. TIME

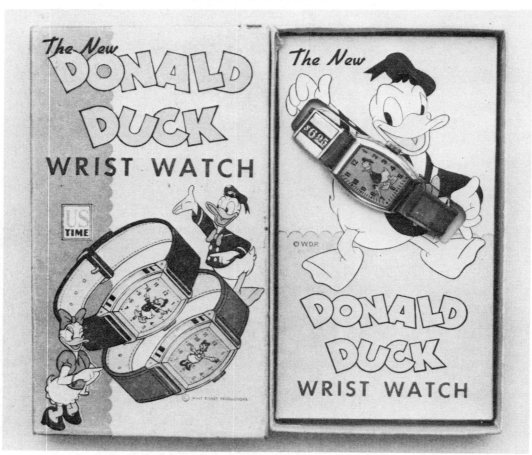

Good – $25; Very Good/Fine – $75; Mint – $125; Mint in Box – $250

DONALD DUCK (DELUXE)
1947 – U.S. TIME

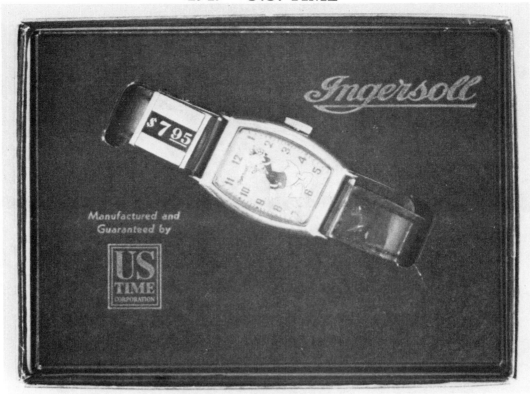

Gold-tone case watch originally sold for $1 more than regular version. Extremely rare today.
Good – $25; Very Good/Fine – $75; Mint – $125; Mint in Box – $175

DONALD DUCK
1948 – INGERSOLL (U.S. TIME)

One of the ten "Birthday Series" watches to celebrate Mickey's 20th Birthday.
Good – $30; Very Good/Fine – $90; Mint – $150; Mint in Box – $275

DONALD DUCK
1955 – U.S. TIME

Colorfully decorated "pop-up" box features a cut-out figure of Donald wearing his own watch. Rare.
Good – $20; Very Good/Fine – $60; Mint – $100; Mint in Box – $175

DOPEY
1948 – INGERSOLL (U.S. TIME)

One of the ten ''Birthday Series'' watches to celebrate Mickey's 20th Birthday.
Good – $25; Very Good/Fine – $75; Mint – $125; **Mint in Box – $250**

GENE AUTRY

1948 – WILANE

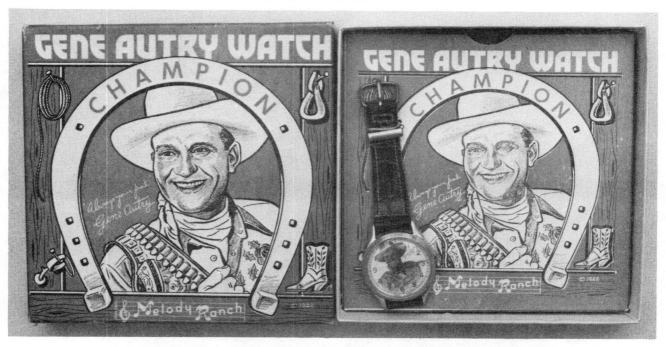

Good – $25; Very Good/Fine – $75; Mint – $125; Mint in Box – $250

GENE AUTRY

1951 – NEW HAVEN

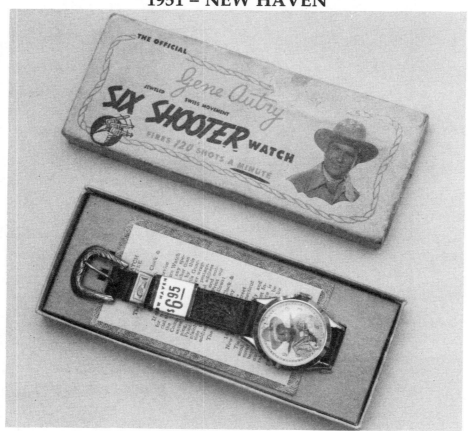

Animated watch features Gene's gun moving back and forth – "120 shots a minute" according to the box.
Good – $25; Very Good/Fine – $75; Mint – $125; Mint in Box – $175

GOOFY
1972 – HELBROS

Unusual "backwards" watch – both numbers and hands run backwards. It really is a "goofy" watch! Beautifully lithographed, colorful dial. 17-jewel movement. Original $19.95 "sticker shock" price and market miscalculation caused Helbros to discontinue it after a short production run. Recent publicity has caused a new surge of demand and prices have been steadily rising due to extremely limited supply.

Good – $37; Very Good/Fine – $111; Mint – $185; Mint in Box – $225

HOPALONG CASSIDY

1950 – U.S. TIME

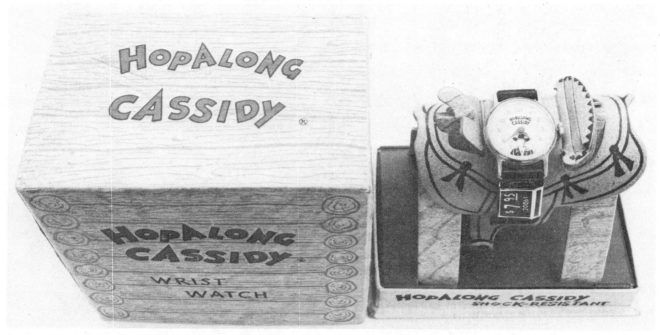

Metal watch was produced continuously for 8 years. Very common. "Saddle Stand" box is also common.
Good – $10; Very Good/Fine – $30; Mint – $50; Mint in Box – $135

HOPALONG CASSIDY

1950 – U.S. TIME

This version features a plastic watch.

Good – $8; Very Good/Fine – $24; Mint – $40; Mint in Box – $135

HOPALONG CASSIDY

1950 – U.S. TIME

Good – $35; Very Good/Fine – $105; Mint – $175; Mint in Box – $275

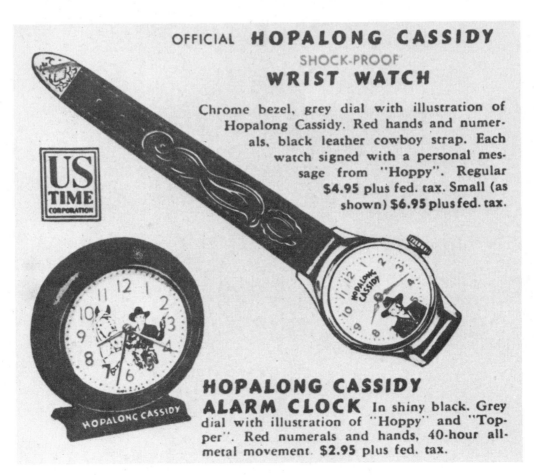

OFFICIAL **HOPALONG CASSIDY**
SHOCK-PROOF
WRIST WATCH

Chrome bezel, grey dial with illustration of Hopalong Cassidy. Red hands and numerals, black leather cowboy strap. Each watch signed with a personal message from "Hoppy". Regular **$4.95** plus fed. tax. Small (as shown) **$6.95** plus fed. tax.

HOPALONG CASSIDY ALARM CLOCK In shiny black. Grey dial with illustration of "Hoppy" and "Topper". Red numerals and hands, 40-hour all-metal movement. **$2.95** plus fed. tax.

Appeared in LIFE magazine issue of December 4, 1950

HOPALONG CASSIDY
1950 – U.S. TIME

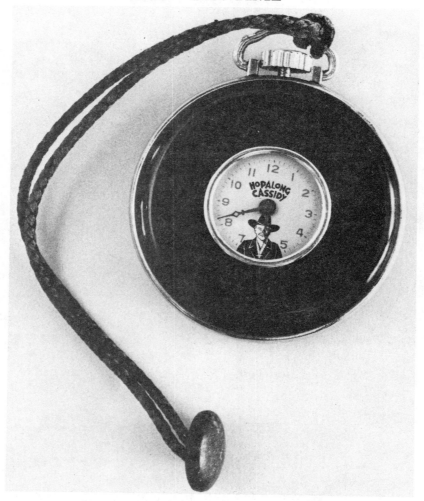

Good – $35; Very Good/Fine – $105; Mint – $175; Mint in Box – $250

HOPALONG CASSIDY

1950 – U.S. TIME

Small-size watch in uncommon box variation.
Good – $10; Very Good/Fine – $30; Mint – $50; Mint in Box – $150

"Regular size" watch originally sold for $2 less than "small size." Collectors today consider this version "large" and attach a slight premium to it.
Good – $15; Very Good/Fine – $45; Mint – $75; Mint in Box – $175

HOWDY DOODY
1954 – PATENT WATCH CO.

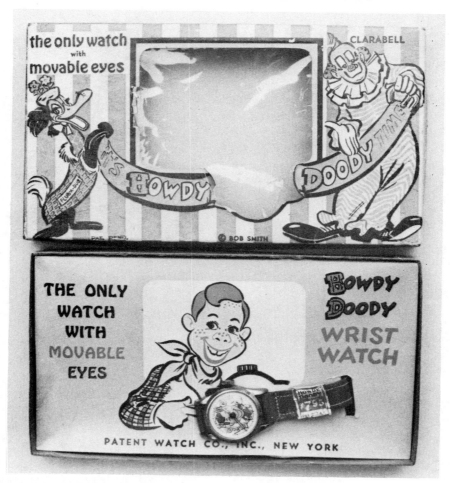

"Moving eyes" watch is scarce. Box is rare.

Good – $20; Very Good/Fine – $60; Mint – $100; Mint in Box – $250

HOWDY DOODY
1954 – INGRAHAM

Watch is scarce. Unique display box is rare.

Good – $20; Very Good/Fine – $60; Mint – $100; **Mint in Box – $250**

JEFF ARNOLD
1953 – INGERSOLL LTD.

Animated: Jeff's right hand with pistol moves up and down. Jeff Arnold is England's most famous cowboy, equivalent to our Hopalong Cassidy or Roy Rogers.

Good – $55; Very Good/Fine – $165; Mint – $275; Mint in Box – $325

JOE CARIOCA
1953 – INGERSOLL (U.S. TIME)

One of the ten "Birthday Series" watches produced to celebrate Mickey's 20th Birthday.
Good – $25; Very Good/Fine – $75; Mint – $125; Mint in Box – $250

JOE PALOOKA
1947 – NEW HAVEN

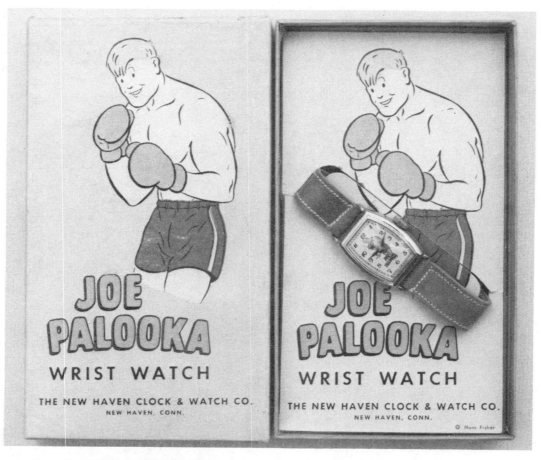

Good – $30; Very Good/Fine – $90; Mint – $150; Mint in Box – $250

LI'L ABNER
1947 – NEW HAVEN

Animated "Movin' Mule" rocks back and forth.

Good – $20; Very Good/Fine – $60; Mint – $100; Mint in Box – $175

LI'L ABNER
1947 – NEW HAVEN

Animated "Waving Flag" moves back and forth.

Good – $20; Very Good/Fine – $60; Mint – $100; Mint in Box – $175

LONE RANGER

1939 – NEW HAVEN

Good – $40; Very Good/Fine – $120; Mint – $200; Mint in Box – $350

LONE RANGER
1939 – NEW HAVEN

Large-size pre-war watch is scarce.
Box is very rare.

Good – $35; Very Good/Fine – $105;
Mint – $175; Mint in Box – $250

LITTLE PIG
1947 – U.S. TIME

Fiddler Pig watch is uncommon. Box is very rare.

Good – $25; Very Good/Fine – $75; Mint – $125; Mint in Box – $250

MARY MARVEL
1948 – FAWCETT

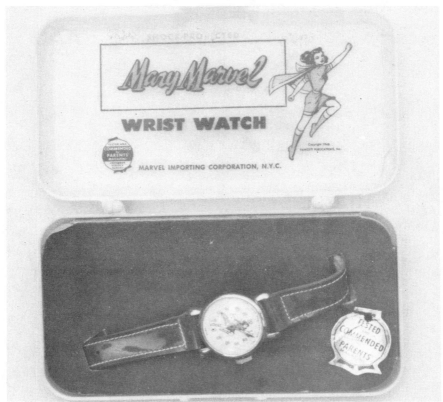

Plastic box is uncommon.
Good – $20; Very Good/Fine – $60; Mint – $100; Mint in Box – $225

Good – $20; Very Good/Fine – $60; Mint – $100; Mint in Box – $200

MICKEY MOUSE
1933 – INGERSOLL

Electric clock features a revolving Mickey. Colorfully decorated strip around top and sides contains the popular Disney characters. Rare clock, extremely rare box.

Good – $100; Very Good/Fine – $300; Mint – $500; Mint in Box – $700

MICKEY MOUSE
(left) 1933 – INGERSOLL   (right) 1934 – INGERSOLL

As part of its first line, Ingersoll introduced a wind-up clock. Although it sold well, the company realized it had made a mistake – no alarm. So, the following year, they introduced an animated alarm clock (right), designing a special movement for Mickey's wagging head. Unfortunately, these proved difficult to maintain and repair, and most were simply thrown away. Both clocks are rare.

(left): Good – $90; Very Good/Fine – $270; Mint – $450; Mint in Box – $600
(right): Good – $60; Very Good/Fine – $180; Mint – $300; Mint in Box – $450

MICKEY MOUSE
1947 – INGERSOLL (U.S. TIME)

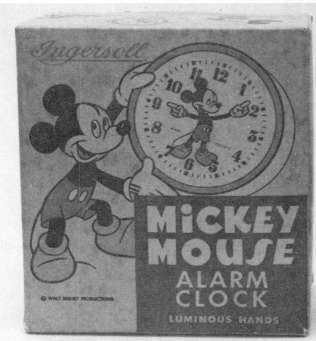

Metal case clock is somewhat rare. Box is rare.

Good – $25; Very Good/Fine – $75; Mint – $125; Mint in Box – $250

MICKEY MOUSE
1949 – INGERSOLL (U.S. TIME)

Plastic case clock is fairly rare. Box is rare.

Good – $25; Very Good/Fine – $75; Mint – $125; Mint in Box – $250

MICKEY MOUSE
1964 – BAYARD

One of a series of Disney clocks made in France. Limited U.S. distribution. Animated: Mickey's head wags back and forth.

Good – $20; Very Good/Fine – $60; Mint – $100; Mint in Box – $125

MICKEY MOUSE
1979 – BRADLEY

Recent alarm clock looks like an oversized pocket watch. Unusual.

Good – $5; Very Good/Fine – $15; Mint – $25; Mint in Box – $35

MICKEY MOUSE
1979 – BRADLEY

Animated clock features all the Disney characters marching around the "Magic Castle." Unusual and scarce.
Good – $10; Very Good/Fine – $30; Mint – $50; Mint in Box – $65

MICKEY MOUSE
1983 – BRADLEY

Recent animated alarm clock features Mickey's feet moving back and forth.

Good – $5; Very Good/Fine – $15; Mint – $25; Mint in Box – $35

MICKEY MOUSE
1933 – INGERSOLL

Second hand features three Mickeys chasing each other. Fairly common. Must have die-debossed back to be completely original. Beware of fakes.
Good – $55; Very Good/Fine – $165; Mint – $275; Mint in Box – $400

MICKEY MOUSE
1933 – INGERSOLL

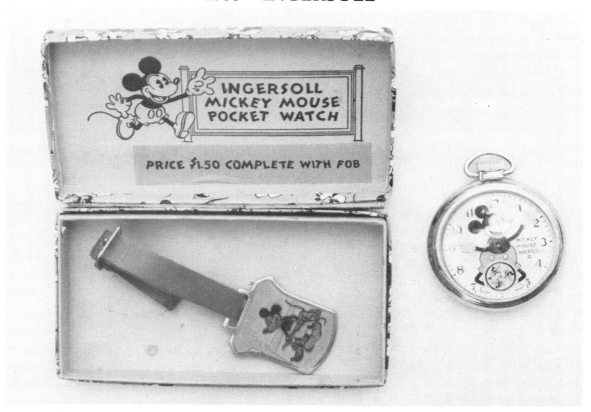

This is a box variation, with a different fob as well.

Good – $55; Very Good/Fine – $165; Mint – $275; Mint in Box – $400

MICKEY MOUSE

Shown here are the two versions of the Mickey Mouse pocket watch. The earlier one, on the left, is slightly larger and has a longer stem. The one on the right is slightly smaller and has a short stem. Collectors attach no particular premium to either model.

MICKEY MOUSE
1934 – INGERSOLL LTD.

With the rousing success of its Mickey timepieces in the U.S., Ingersoll authorized its English affiliate to produce timepieces as well. These have the word ''Foreign'' under the ''6'' to differentiate them from the U.S. version. Apparently the English designer couldn't make a decision about the best Mickey portrayal, so there are two different versions. Extremely rare.

Good – $100; Very Good/Fine – $300; Mint – $500; Mint in Box – $750

MICKEY MOUSE
1938 – INGERSOLL

Considered by many Disney collectors to be one of the most beautiful and desirable of all Mickey watches. Extremely rare. Must have Mickey decal on back to be completely original. Box is ultra-rare: less than ten known to exist.

Good – $95; Very Good/Fine – $285; Mint – $475; Mint in Box – $675

MICKEY MOUSE
1976 – BRADLEY

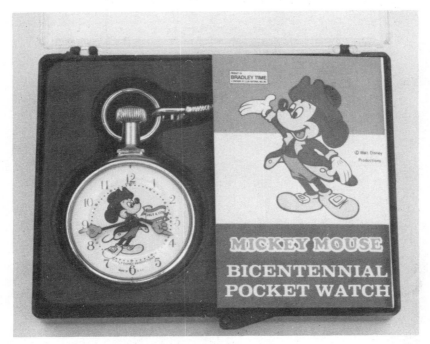

Good – $8; Very Good/Fine – $24; Mint – $40; Mint in Box – $50

1939 Sears Advertisements

(L-R) Snow White (1939—Ingersoll), Snow White "Magic Mirror" box (1950—U.S. TIME)

Mickey Mouse and Minnie Mouse "statue" watches (1958—Timex)

Cinderella wristwatch in glass slipper (1950—U.S. TIME)

Mickey Mouse wristwatch in "Birthday Cake" package (1947—U.S. TIME)

◀ Original store display
for Woody Woodpecker animated
alarm clock
(1950—Columbia Time)

Mickey Mouse store display ▶
(c. 1973)

Mickey Mouse wristwatch in colorful "presentation box" (1952—U.S. TIME)

Mickey Mouse lapel watch (1938—Ingersoll)

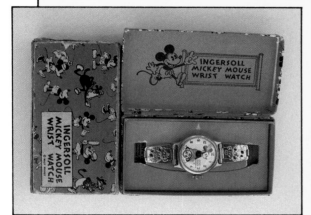

The watch that started it all— the famous "Mickey Number One" (1933-Ingersoll)

Pluto and Mickey Mouse alarm clocks, produced in France (1964-Bayard)

Donald Duck and Mickey Mouse wristwatches in unusual "pop-up" display boxes (1955—U.S. TIME)

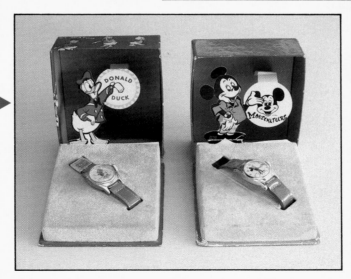

(top) Betty Boop pocket watch (1934—Ingraham)
(bottom) Donald Duck pocket watch
(1939—Ingersoll)

Bugs Bunny animated alarm clock
(1951—Ingraham), Charlie McCarthy
animated alarm clock
(1938—Gilbert)

Three Little Pigs alarm clock
(1934—Ingersoll)

Three Little Pigs pocket watch
with fob (1934—Ingersoll)

Some Pig friends: Porky
(1949—Ingraham),
Little (Fiddler)
(1947—U.S. TIME)

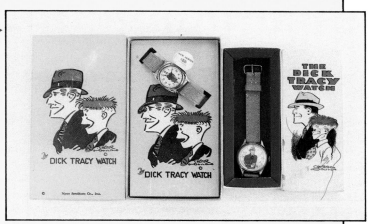

L-R; Dick Tracy wristwatch ▶
(1948—New Haven),
Dick Tracy animated wristwatch
(1951—New Haven)

▲
Goofy (1972—Helbros)

Davy Crockett wristwatch ▶
in "powder horn" package
(1954—U.S. TIME)

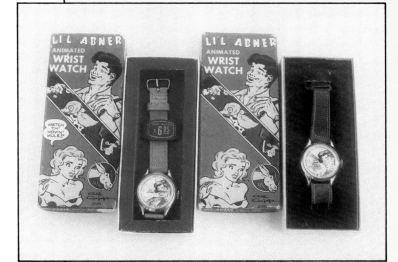

▲
Li'l Abner
(1947-New Haven)

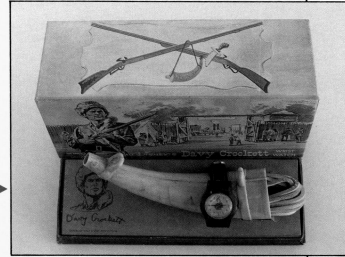

(top) Popeye pocket watch ▶
(1934—New Haven)
(bottom) Popeye pocket watch
(1935—New Haven)

Buck Rogers pocket
watch (1935—Ingraham)

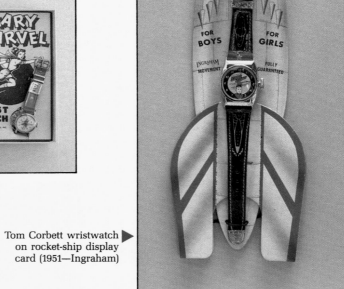

Capt. Marvel, Mary Marvel
(both 1948—Fawcett)

Tom Corbett wristwatch
on rocket-ship display
card (1951—Ingraham) ▶

Buzz Corey
(1951—U.S.
TIME), Capt.
Liberty (1951—
Liberty Watch
Co.) ▶

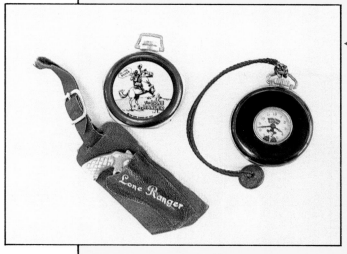

L-R; Lone Ranger pocket watch with fob (1939—New Haven), Hopalong Cassidy pocket watch and lapel cord (1950—U.S. TIME)

L-R; Hopalong Cassidy wristwatches: regular size, large size (1950—U.S. TIME)

Superman (1939—New Haven), Joe Palooka (1947—New Haven)

Roy Rogers alarm clock (1951—Ingraham)

Tom Mix pocket watch with fob (1934—Ingersoll)

Ingersoll store display (L-R)
Mickey Mouse Deluxe (1947),
Mickey Mouse (1949), Daisy (1948),
Donald Duck (1947), Mickey Mouse
(1946), Donald Duck (1947)

MICKEY MOUSE

1933 – INGERSOLL

The watch that started it all – the famous ''Mickey Number One.'' Small second hand features three Mickey's chasing each other. Also came with a leather band. Metal band shown is more desirable.

Good – $40; Very Good/Fine – $120; Mint – $200; Mint in Box – $325

MICKEY MOUSE (DELUXE)
1938 – INGERSOLL

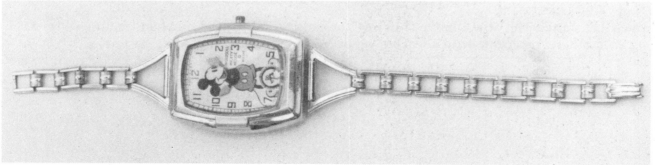

Features one Mickey on the second hand. Girl's version came with a small bracelet and charms. Extremely rare box.

Good – $30; Very Good/Fine – $90; Mint – $150; Mint in Box – $300

MICKEY MOUSE
1939 – INGERSOLL

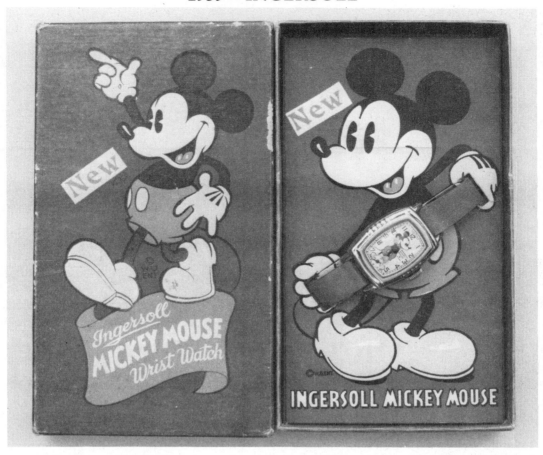

Notice that the Mickey second hand has now been replaced by a conventional second hand.

Good – $25; Very Good/Fine – $75; Mint – $125; Mint in Box – $250

MICKEY MOUSE **$2**⁶⁹

A $2.95 Value

"Mickey," in gay enameled colors, keeps track of the time by moving his hands. The little movie star always tells correct time. The sturdy cases are chromium plated with unbreakable crystals. On the second hand dial, three colored Mickeys are chasing each other in a circle. Mickey also appears on each side of the wrist bands. Make your kiddie happy! Shpg. wt., 8 oz.
4 D 1664—Metal Band
4 D 1665—Leather Strap. **$2.69**

Mickey Mouse Watch and Fob!

On the dial is Mickey Mouse in gay colors. For a second hand, same as on the wrist watch, there are three Mickeys chasing each other in a circle—Mickey is on back of the watch and on fob, too. Nickel plated case with leather fob to match. Regularly $1.50. Shpg. wt., 8 oz.
4 D 1603......... **$1.39**

1937 Sears Advertisement

63

MICKEY MOUSE
1946 – KELTON (U.S. TIME)

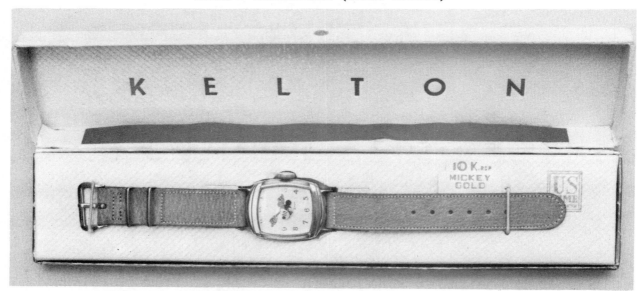

First post-war Mickey watch is extremely rare due to limited production.
Good – $25; Very Good/Fine – $75; Mint – $125; Mint in Box – $175

MICKEY MOUSE
1947 – INGERSOLL (U.S. TIME)

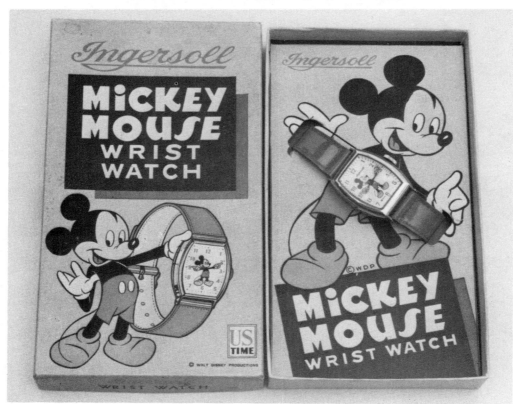

Watch is quite common.
Good – $15; Very Good/Fine – $45; Mint – $75; Mint in Box – $200

MICKEY MOUSE
1947 – U.S. TIME

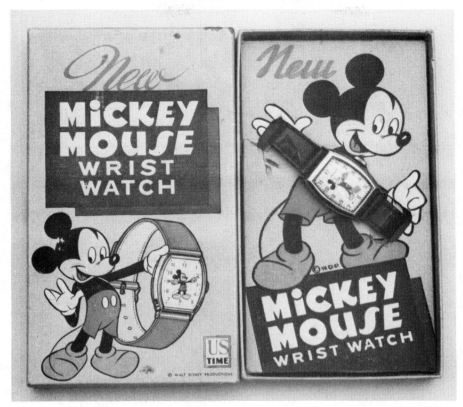

Note that the word "Ingersoll" has been replaced by the word "New" on the top of both the box and insert.
Good – $15; Very Good/Fine – $45; Mint – $75; Mint in Box – $200

MICKEY MOUSE
1947 – U.S. TIME

Gold-tone case originally sold for $1 more than regular version. Extremely rare today.
Good – $20; Very Good/Fine – $60; Mint – $100; Mint in Box – $175

MICKEY MOUSE
1947 – U.S. TIME

This "special package" sold for $10.95 and came with a pen and ring, in addition to the watch. The "Birthday Cake" package served a dual purpose: it celebrated Mickey's 20th Birthday, and, by putting candles on top (see color photo), it was a ready-made gift for a youngster. Packaging is extremely rare.

Good – $15; Very Good/Fine – $45; Mint – $75; Mint in Box – $200

MICKEY MOUSE
1950 – INGERSOLL (U.S. TIME)

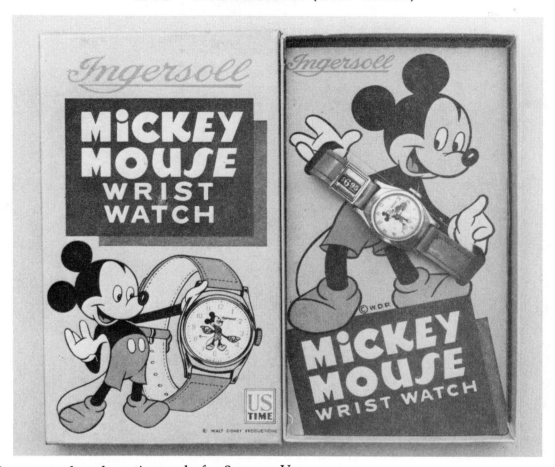

Metal watch was produced continuously for 8 years. Very common.
Good – $10; Very Good/Fine – $30; Mint – $50; Mint in Box – $200

MICKEY MOUSE
1952 – U.S. TIME

Colorful "presentation box" is uncommon.

Good – $10; Very Good/Fine – $30; Mint – $50; Mint in Box – $200

MICKEY MOUSE
1978 – BRADLEY

Issued to celebrate Mickey's 50th Birthday. (L-R) Woman's, man's, child's.

Good – $8; Very Good/Fine – $24; Mint – $40; Mint in Box – $75

MICKEY MOUSE

1955 – U.S. TIME

"Pop-up" box features a cut-out figure of Mickey wearing his own watch.

Good – $10; Very Good/Fine – $30; Mint – $50; Mint in Box – $175

MICKEY MOUSE
1958 – U.S. TIME

Statue on left is porcelain, statue on right is plastic. Note that on left watch, poor Mickey has been taken off his own watch and replaced by the words "Mickey Mouse."

Good – $10; Very Good/Fine – $30; Mint – $50; Mint in Box – $150

MICKEY MOUSE
1968 – TIMEX

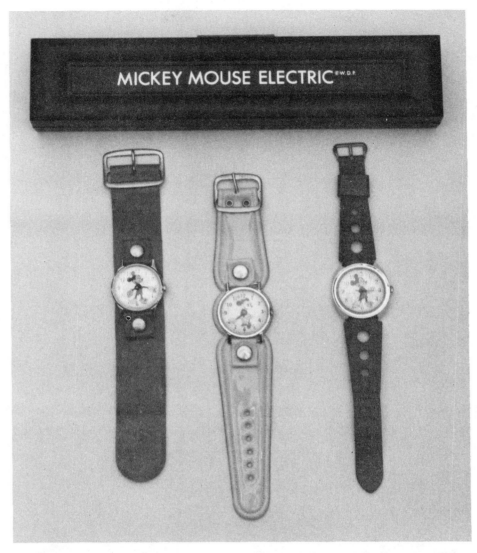

Left and center watches are wind-ups (Mickey and Minnie), right watch is electric. Electric model is highly sought.

(left and center watches): Good –$10; Very Good/Fine – $30; Mint – $50; Mint in Box – $100
(right): Good –$25; Very Good/Fine – $75; Mint – $125; Mint in Box – $175

MICKEY MOUSE
1982 – BRADLEY

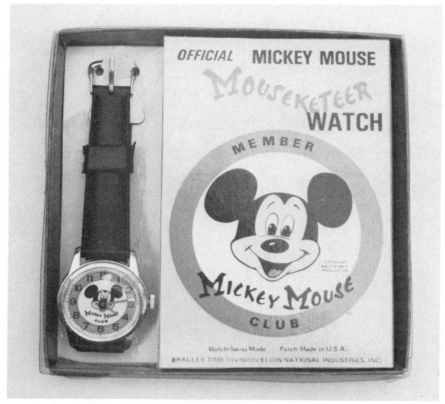

Issued to coincide with the attempted TV revival of the Mickey Mouse Club in 1982.
Good – $5; Very Good/Fine – $15; Mint – $25; Mint in Box – $40

MICKEY MOUSE
1983 – BRADLEY

Commemorates the 50th Anniversary of the Mickey Mouse wristwatch. Limited production and selective distribution have made this watch an ''instant collectible.'' After-market prices have risen steadily.
Good –$20; Very Good/Fine – $60; Mint – $100; Mint in Box – $150

MICKEY MOUSE AND FRIENDS

(L-R) Raised Mickey figure in gold, Epcot Center, "see-through movement," Tokyo Disneyland, Disneyland.
A selection of recent Bradley watches. Because they were limited both in production and distribution, it is entirely possible that they may become desirable collectibles in the future. By purchasing contemporary timepieces that you personally like, you are laying the groundwork for your future collection!

MINNIE MOUSE
1958 – U.S. TIME

First appearance of Minnie on a timepiece.

Good – $10; Very Good/Fine – $30; Mint – $50; Mint in Box – $100

Mickey Mouse Time Mug from the 1950s. **Value: $25-35**

Timex promo piece for the 1968 Mickey Watch

Here's something any collector would give his eye-teeth for! This store display features a giant 6-foot wide Mickey pocket watch held over the sales counter by four wooden Mickey cut-outs, each 3-feet high. Picture was taken February 26, 1935 at the Marshall-Field's department store in Chicago. Does it still exist somewhere?

NEW MICKEY MOUSE
Alarm Clock

On the dial is an animated Mickey Mouse head wagging, hands pointing the time. Choice of red or green case. Packed in a self-display carton which makes selling easy. $1.50 retail, $1.05 trade.

MICKEY MOUSE DISPLAY

—a sure attention-getter for your windows. Also valuable as a counter sales-card. Places on it for 3 pocket watches and 2 wrist watches. FREE DISPLAY.

INGERSOLL MICKEY MOUSE
POCKET WATCH AND FOB—

complete in a colorful gift box. Mickey's own hands point the time, getting into comical positions doing so. It's the watch sensation of the decade and a wonderful value at $1.50 retail. $1.05 trade.

INGERSOLL MICKEY MOUSE
WRIST WATCH—

with Mickey's hands telling the time. A million have already been sold—more millions will be. Leather band or metal Mickey Mouse strap. $3.75 retail. $2.50 trade.

Trade ad from 1933 Disney Merchandise Catalogue

Trade ad from 1935 Disney Merchandise Catalogue

Genuine MICKEY MOUSE Watches

YOUR CHOICE $2.98 EACH

Watch illustrations ¾ Actual Size

$1.39 IN GIFT BOX

Mickey Mouse Watch and Fob
Unbreakable Crystal

An Improved, Smaller Size, Better Model, Mickey Mouse Watch than the Regular Mickey Watches sold!

YOUR BOY will get a lot of things when he owns a Mickey Mouse watch. Genuine thin model Ingersoll—on the dial is Mickey Mouse in gay colors telling you the time with his hands. For a second hand there are three Little Mickeys chasing each other in a circle. Mickeys on the back of the watch, too. And when the watch is in his pocket, Mickey's there, chipper as you please, dangling at the end of the "grown up" looking fob. Nickel plated case. Shpg. wt. 6 oz. .... 4 F 1650 .... $1.39

Mickey Mouse Wrist Watch
Regular $3.75 Value
Big Saving When You Buy at Sears.

Mickey Mouse on a wrist watch! Can you think of anything to please a child more? On the dial is Mickey Mouse in all his glory telling you the time with his hands. For a second hand, three Junior Mickeys chase around in a circle. Two Mickey Mouse characters in enameled colors on the wrist band. Genuine Ingersoll. Chromium plated case unbreakable crystal. White dial with black figures. Shpg. wt. 6 oz.

Metal Band. 4 F 950...$2.98	Leather Band 4 F 951...$2.98

Mickey Mouse Alarm Clock

No trick getting up mornings with Mickey Mouse on the job to waken you. Mickey Mouse with his head wagging tells time with his hands. Genuine Ingersoll clock. 30-hour movement. Attractive red or green finish. State color wanted. 4⅜ in. high. Has 3⅝ in. dial. Shpg. wt., 1 lb. 8 oz. 5 F 8518...$1.39

$2.79

American Made Popular Size Laddie Wrist Watches

Regular $3.50 Laddie Watch. Extremely popular; artistic in shape. Chromium plated case, plain dial. Made exclusively for *Sears*. A good timekeeper. Shpg. wt., 8 oz. Open link Chromium plated band.

Metal Band 4 F 1702 $2.79	Leather wristband 4 F 1703...$2.79

For above with luminous dial add 40c.

$1.89

Official Boy Scout Watches

...Around the dial are inscribed the 12 scout laws, while the minute hand points to them with this inscription: "A Scout Is." On the hour hand is the scout motto: "Be Prepared." Chromium plated cases and non-breakable crystals. Made by Ingersoll. Shpg. wt., each, 6 oz.

Pocket Watch	Wrist Watch
Official colors on dial and hands.	Official colors on dial and hands. Leather Strap.
	Plain Dial 4 F 912 ...... $3.39
4 F 1652	
Thin model.. $1.89	Luminous dial 4 F 913 ...... 3.89

WHO'S AFRAID OF THE BIG BAD WOLF

Big Bad Wolf Wrist Watch—*$3.75 Value*

With each tick of the watch the Bad Wolf's evil eye is winking at the three little pigs on a bright colored dial. Center opening metal wrist band; decorated with Bad Wolf and Little Pigs. Thin model Chromium plated case. Nonbreakable crystal. Stem wind and stem set. Made by Ingersoll. Shpg. wt., 6 oz.

Metal Band 4 F 952 $2.98	Leather Band 4 F 953 $2.98

Big Bad Wolf Watch and Fob

With each tick of the watch the Bad Wolf winks at Three Little Pigs on bright colored dial. Dangling from black leather strap is a nickel plated fob with Three Pigs in bright colors. Message from Walt Disney on back of watch. Ingersoll, thin model nickel-plated case. Unbreakable crystal. Shpg. wt., 6 oz.
4 F 1651.........$1.39

Big Bad Wolf Alarm Clock

Three Little Pigs Alarm Clock. Ferocious jaws of Bad Wolf open and close with each tick of the clock. Bright red case and dial; little pigs and bad wolf in lifelike colors. Genuine Ingersoll 30-hour movement model. Case 4⅜ in. high with 3⅝-in. dial. Shpg. wt., 1 lb. 8 oz. 5 F 8519.........$1.39

$2.39

Genuine Ingraham Popular Priced Wrist Watch

Handsome watches in stunning Chromium plated cases. Good timekeeper, too. Ingraham American made. Neat, plain pattern case and band. Raised gilt numerals. Shpg. wt., ea., 8 oz.

Open Link Metal Band 4 F 1700 $2.39	Leather Strap 4 F 1701 $2.39

Great News for the Youngster
Orphan Annie and Dick Tracy Wrist Watches
Made to Sell for $3.95

All the boys and girls are wearing them . . . prize them beyond words. American movement. A fully guaranteed timekeeper. Chromium plated cases. Genuine leather strap. Shpg. wt., each, 8 oz.

Orphan Annie

Annie's picture in colors on the dial. The ideal watch for the young American Miss who wants the latest. In attractive Orphan Annie box.
4 F 1715 $3.59

Dick Tracy

Sears is right up to the minute with this genuine American Dick Tracy Wrist Watch. Has an official reproduction of Dick Tracy himself in colors on the dial.
4 F 1714... $3.59

QUALITY First—QUALITY Always—at *Sears*

1934 Sears Advertisement

"Look, Grandpa— we've got Ingersolls, too!"

Appeared in LIFE magazine issue of December 8, 1952

For Christmas

GRAND FUN FOR THE KIDS— AND A GREAT WATCH, TOO

Ask Grandfather about Ingersoll—he's known it a life-time. Ingersoll's the *ideal* gift for kids and grown-ups, too. Its super-accurate movement takes a licking, yet keeps on ticking. *And you just can't beat the prices.*

"CINDERELLA"...... in the "Slipper" Gift Box ... $6.95

"SNOW WHITE" .... in the "Magic Mirror" Box ... $6.95

"MICKEY MOUSE".....in the "Presentation" Gift Box .. $6.95

"HOPALONG CASSIDY"... in "Saddle Stand" Box .. $6.95

give "the most famous name in time"

a product of the UNITED STATES TIME CORPORATION
World's Largest Manufacturer of Wrist Watches

ORPHAN ANNIE
1935 – NEW HAVEN

This large-size early version is uncommon.
Good –$25; Very Good/Fine – $75; Mint – $125; Mint in Box – $250

ORPHAN ANNIE
1948 – NEW HAVEN

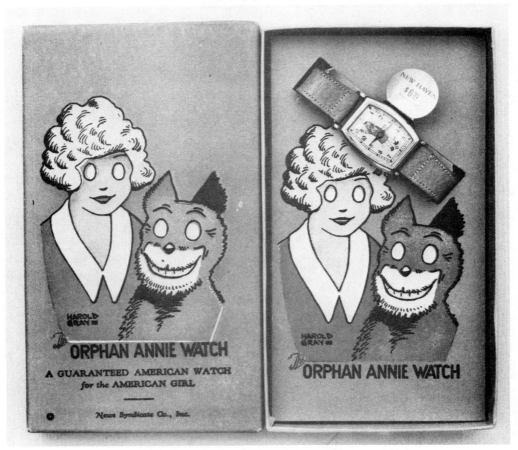

This watch is smaller than the 1935 version.
Good –$20; Very Good/Fine – $60; Mint – $100; Mint in Box – $175

PINOCCHIO
1964 – BAYARD

One of a series of Disney clocks produced in France. Limited U.S. distribution. Animated: Jiminy Cricket dances above Pinocchio's head.

Good – $15; Very Good/Fine – $45; Mint – $75; Mint in Box – $100

PINOCCHIO
1948 – INGERSOLL

One of the ten ''Birthday Series'' watches produced to celebrate Mickey's 20th Birthday.
Good – $25; Very Good/Fine – $75; Mint – $125; Mint in Box – $250

PINOCCHIO
1948 – U.S. TIME

Unusual ''Birthday Cake'' package sold for $10.95, complete with a pen and ring. Extremely rare.
Good – $25; Very Good/Fine – $75; Mint – $125; Mint in Box – $250

PLUTO
1964 – BAYARD

One of a series of Disney clocks produced in France. Limited U.S. distribution. Animated: Pluto's head wags back and forth.

Good – $15; Very Good/Fine – $45; Mint – $75; Mint in Box – $100

POPEYE
1968 – SMITHS

Made in England. Animated: Sweetpea's head moves back and forth.
Good –$25; Very Good/Fine – $75; Mint – $125; Mint in Box – $150

POPEYE
1934 – NEW HAVEN

Colorfully decorated with all the Thimble Theater characters. Second hand features Wimpy eternally chasing a hamburger. Rare.
Good – $70; Very Good/Fine – $210; Mint – $350; Mint in Box – $450

POPEYE
1935 – NEW HAVEN

Apparently the New Haven folks felt their 1934 version was "too busy" with all the characters on it. This is the "sanitized" result.
Good – $60; Very Good/Fine – $180; Mint – $300; Mint in Box – $400

POPEYE
1935 – NEW HAVEN

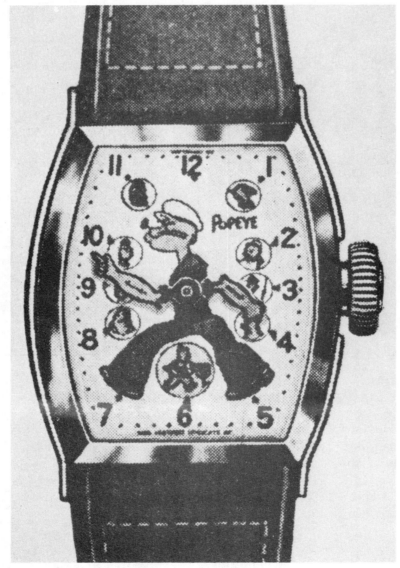

Extremely scarce watch. Very rare box.

Good – $45; Very Good/Fine – $135; Mint – $225; Mint in Box – $350

POPEYE
c. 1948 – MANUFACTURER UNKNOWN

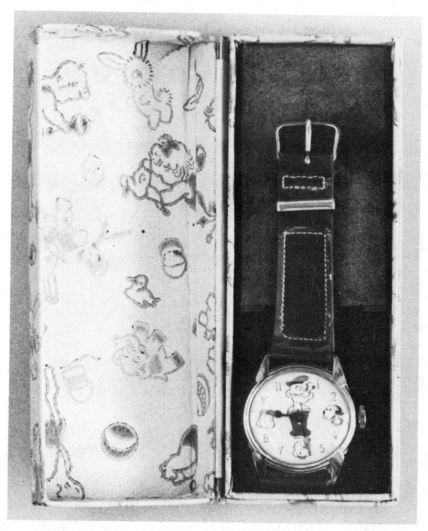

This appears to be a ''knock-off'' watch originally made in the late 1940s. Neither the watch nor box contain any copyright notice or manufacturer's information. However, we have seen several of these watches in the identical box, so this is apparently a production item.

Good – $25; Very Good/Fine – $75; Mint – $125; Mint in Box – $150

PORKY PIG
1949 – INGRAHAM

Round case variation.
Good – $20; Very Good/Fine – $60; Mint – $100; Mint in Box – $200

Square case version. Note the box picture has been changed to indicate this.
Good – $20; Very Good/Fine – $60; Mint – $100; Mint in Box – $200

PUSS-N-BOOTS
1949 – NUHOPE

Good – $10; Very Good/Fine – $30; Mint – $50; Mint in Box – $100

ROBIN
1978 – TIMEX

Produced in Canada, received limited U.S. distribution.

Good – $7; Very Good/Fine – $21; Mint – $35; Mint in Box – $50

ROBIN HOOD

1938 – VIKING

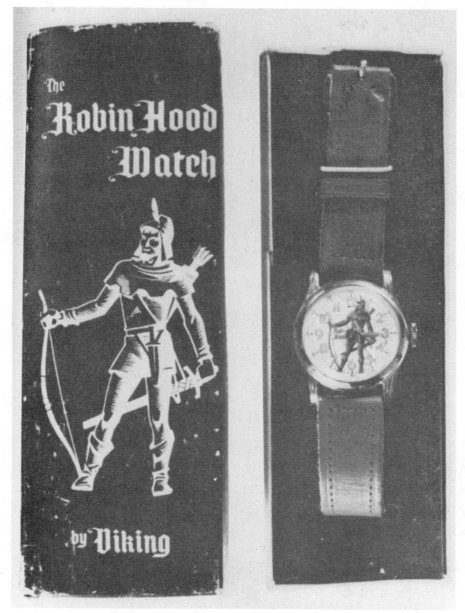

Good – $20; Very Good/Fine – $60; Mint – $100; Mint in Box – $150

ROBIN HOOD
1956 – BRADLEY

''3-D'' pop-up box features Robin Hood with his Merry Men in Sherwood Forest. Unique box is rare.
Good – $10; Very Good/Fine – $30; Mint – $50; Mint in Box – $75

ROCKY JONES
1954 – INGRAHAM

Good – $25; Very Good/Fine – $75; Mint – $125; Mint in Box – $250

ROY ROGERS
1951 – INGRAHAM

Animated: Roy and Trigger gallop back and forth. Extremely common clock comes in a variety of colors: "desert sand," "sky blue," and "cactus green." Boxes are also common.

Good – $15; Very Good/Fine – $45; Mint – $75; Mint in Box – $125

ROY ROGERS
1959 – BRADLEY

Good – $25; Very Good/Fine – $75; Mint – $125; Mint in Box – $175

ROY ROGERS
1951 – INGRAHAM

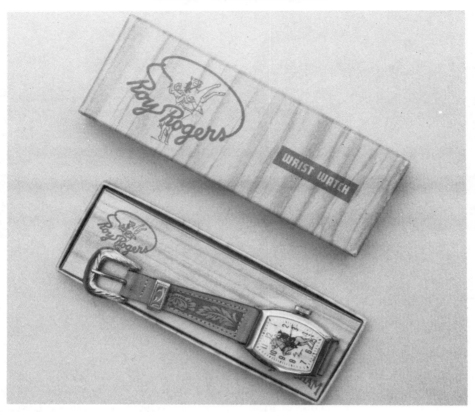

This version features Roy on a rearing Trigger.

Good – $15; Very Good/Fine – $45; Mint – $75; Mint in Box – $150

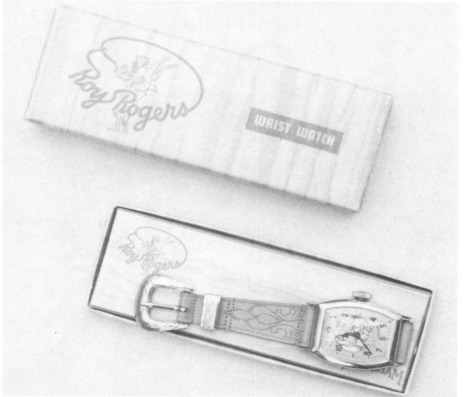

This version features Roy and Trigger posing.

Good – $15; Very Good/Fine – $45; Mint – $75; Mint in Box – $150

ROY ROGERS
1951 – INGRAHAM

"Posing" watch with expansion bracelet in "presentation" box.
Good – $15; Very Good/Fine – $45; Mint – $75; Mint in Box – $150

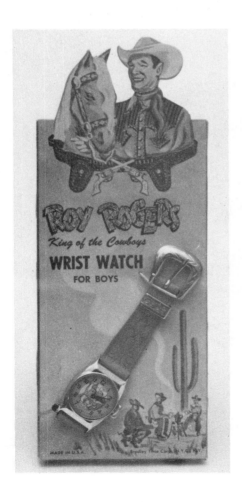

ROY ROGERS
1951 – INGRAHAM

Round case "posing" watch on a "pop-up" display box. Uncommon.
Good – $15; Very Good/Fine – $45; Mint – $75; Mint in Box – $175

SMITTY
1935 – NEW HAVEN

Watch is rare. Box is very rare.
Good –$35; Very Good/Fine – $105; Mint – $175; Mint in Box – $300

SNOW WHITE
1964 – BAYARD

One of a series of Disney clocks produced in France. Limited U.S. distribution. Animated: Bluebird moves back and forth.

Good – $15; Very Good/Fine – $45; Mint – $75; Mint in Box – $100

SNOW WHITE
1939 – INGERSOLL

Rare large-size pre-war watch. Box top features a scene from the movie on a plastic sheet. Unusual and rare.
Good – $25; Very Good/Fine – $75; Mint – $125; Mint in Box – $200

SNOW WHITE
1950 – U.S. TIME

Metal watch is common. "Magic Mirror" box is scarce.

Good – $8; Very Good/Fine – $24; Mint – $40; Mint in Box – $150

SNOW WHITE
1954 – U.S. TIME

"Figural box" allowed purchaser to punch-out a cardboard figure of Show White.
Good – $8; Very Good/Fine – $24; Mint – $40; Mint in Box – $125

Watch is now plastic. Snow White is now a molded plastic figure which can be removed.
Good – $8; Very Good/Fine – $24; Mint – $40; Mint in Box – $125

SNOW WHITE
1958 – U.S. TIME

Statue on left is porcelain, statue on right is plastic. Note that on left watch, Snow White's picture has been replaced by the words ''Snow White.''

Good – $8; Very Good/Fine – $24; Mint – $40; Mint in Box – $100

SUPERMAN
1959 – BRADLEY

Good – $40; Very Good/Fine – $120; Mint – $200; Mint in Box – $250

SUPERMAN
1939 – NEW HAVEN

Large-size pre-war watch is scarce. Box is very rare.
Good – $40; Very Good/Fine – $120; Mint – $200; Mint in Box – $350

SUPERMAN
1948 – NEW HAVEN

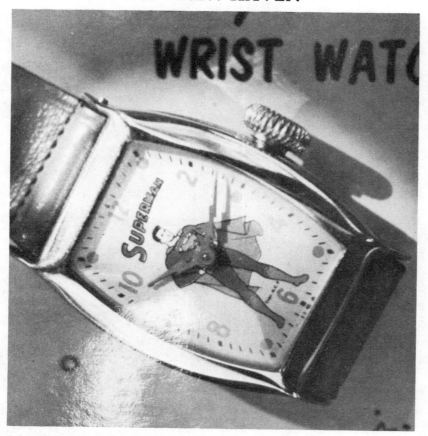

Good – $35; Very Good/Fine – $105; Mint – $175; Mint in Box – $250

SUPERMAN
1976 – TIMEX

Two sizes, large and small. Produced in Canada, received limited distribution in U.S.
Good – $8; Very Good/Fine – $24; Mint – $40; Mint in Box – $50

THREE LITTLE PIGS
1934 – INGERSOLL

Animated: Wolf's jaw opens and closes: Dial should be bright red. Extremely difficult to find in this condition – usually found with a faded (pink) dial. Value is considerably less. Box is ultra-rare: less than 10 known to exist.

Good – $120; Very Good/Fine – $360; Mint – $600; Mint in Box – $800

THREE LITTLE PIGS
1934 – INGERSOLL

Animated: Wolf's eye winks. Dial should be bright red. Must have die-debossed back to be completely original. (See next page.)

Good – $90; Very Good/Fine – $270; Mint – $450; Mint in Box – $700

THREE LITTLE PIGS

Little information is available about this watch. The consensus among the informed dealers and collectors we spoke with was that it most likely is a prototype. Ingersoll may have produced a small number to show to Disney executives, who rejected it in favor of the pocket watch shown on page 109. So few have ever turned up that we are unable to determine a price.

THREE
LITTLE PIGS
1934 – INGERSOLL

Complete watch with decorated wristband is extremely rare and desirable. Dial should be bright red. Box is ultra-rare: less than 10 known to exist. Good – $75; Very Good/Fine – $225; Mint – $375; Mint in Box – $500

INGERSOLL
THREE LITTLE PIGS
ALARM CLOCK

The Big Bad Wolf's hungry jaws open and close in rhythm to the clock tick. It's a great clock and a sure-fire seller. The dial and case are bright red. The display carton in which the clock is packed has original Walt Disney drawings on it. You'll sell a lot of these clocks. $1.50 retail. $1.05 trade.

FREE display card for the 3 Little Pigs Watch. The pigs and wolf drawn by Walt Disney himself. A sure "stopper" for your window.

Ingersoll Three Little Pigs Watch and Fob

The wolf's evil eye is winking. The 3 Little Pigs are right there on the red dial. It's a great watch and you ought to sell a pile of 'em! The back makes the watch a good luck token because it has a personal message from Walt Disney: "May the big bad wolf never come to your door"... But loads of customers will come into your door if you display the watch in your window. $1.50 retail. $1.05 trade.

Trade ad from 1934 Disney Merchandise Catalogue

TOM CORBETT
1951 – INGRAHAM

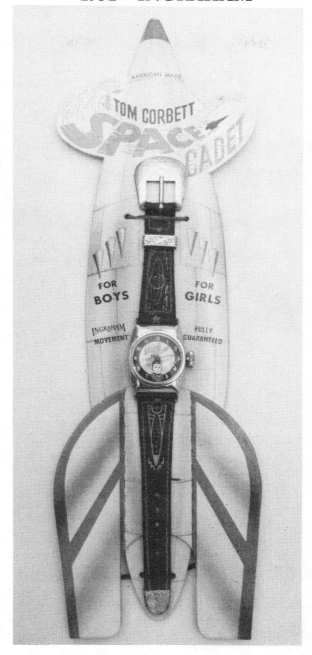

Watch is fairly common. Unique display card package is scarce.

Good – $10; Very Good/Fine – $30; Mint – $50; Mint in Box – $150

TOM MIX

1934 – INGERSOLL

Animated: Second hand features the head of a Texas Longhorn steer. Must have die-debossed back to be completely original. Ultra-rare: less than ten watches known to exist.

Good – $120; Very Good/Fine – $360; Mint – $600; Mint in Box – $800

WOODY WOODPECKER
1950 – COLUMBIA TIME

Animated: Woody's head moves back and forth. Fairly common.

Good – $25; Very Good/Fine – $75; Mint – $125; Mint in Box – $175

WOODY WOODPECKER
1950 – INGRAHAM

Good – $25; Very Good/Fine – $75; Mint – $125; Mint in Box – $200

ZORRO
1957 – U.S. TIME

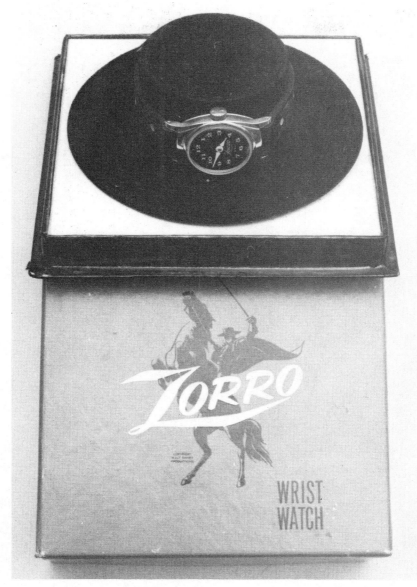

Uninspired watch simply says "Zorro." Sombrero package is scarce.
Good – $5; Very Good/Fine – $15; Mint – $25; Mint in Box – $100

NEW HAVEN
CHARACTER WATCHES

ORPHAN ANNIE

DICK TRACY

SMITTY

IN BRIGHT

SNAPPY COLORS

RIGHT ON THE DIAL

Real timekeepers, thin models, curved backs to fit the wrist, unbreakable crystals, removable leather straps in colors, and silvered dials. Chromium finished case and sturdy, dependable movement.

Orphan Annie is reproduced in Red and Yellow on the dial, and the box is an attractive package in Yellow, Red, Green and Black. Dick Tracy is reproduced in Blue and Red, and the box also has a color scheme of Red and Blue. Smitty is in Green, Red and Black on the dial, and the box is Yellow and Black.

(Manufactured under exclusive license of Famous Artists Syndicate)

INGERSOLL WATCHES

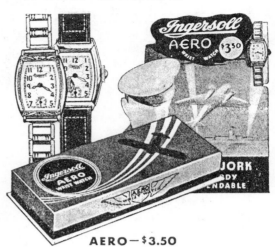

COMPACT—$3.50

Compact can be used as a bag watch, a pocket watch, or a desk clock. Handsomely finished in chromium with two enamel colors . . . red and ivory, black and ivory, or black and green. Fully luminous dial and hands for time telling at night. **Your cost, $2.33.** *Ask for free display.*

AERO—$3.50

Aero is available in two case styles . . . FANCY, delicately embossed, with stainless metal ratchet band . . . PLAIN, slim and smart, with perspiration-proof black leather strap. Silvered dial, luminous hands, unbreakable crystal. Cases plated with durable chromium. **Your cost, $2.45** . . . . *Ask for free display.*

MICKEY LAPEL WATCH—$1.50

Small model finished in black and nickel. Mickey in colors on dial and back. Black lapel cord.
Your cost, $1.05

MICKEY STANDARD WRIST $3.25

The standard wrist watch for children. Sturdy, round movement in strong chromium plated case. Leather strap or metal band available. Colorful gift box. **Your cost, $2.28**

MICKEY MOUSE DELUXE WRIST $3.95

The new, smaller, finer, wrist model. Not too large for the smallest wrist. Rectangular case, chromium finished. Available with metal ratchet band, leather strap or charm bracelet.
Your cost, $2.77

M. M. DELUXE WRIST

M. M. LAPEL   M. M. STANDARD WRIST

MICKEY MOUSE ASSORTMENT

This fine assortment is made up of three Mickey DeLuxe Wrist (one of each, style band), three Mickey Standard Wrist (two metal one leather), and one Mickey Lapel.

You get FREE a clever flasher display (right); seven Mickey Mouse Magazines to give to purchasers of watches. Each box contains a special subscription blank which provides for three extra issues of Mickey Mouse Magazine FREE.

**Your cost is $16.20
You sell it for $23.10**

Watches shown 1/3 size   Terms: 2%, 10 days

From the 1937 Ingersoll sales catalogue

119

THE INGERSOLL-WATERBURY COMPANY
JOBBER'S NET PRICES
Not Subject to Cash Discount
July 1, 1935

Model	Jobber	Retailer 1%	2%	Consumer	Finish
POCKET WATCHES					
Ensign	$ .69	$ .87	$ .88	$1.25	Nickel
Yankee	.83	1.04	1.05	1.50	Chromium
Yankee Radiolite	1.00	1.31	1.33	2.00	Chromium
Mickey Mouse	**.83**	**1.04**	**1.05**	**1.50**	**Nickel**
Junior	1.00	1.31	1.33	2.00	Chromium
WRIST WATCHES					
Aero Plain	1.60	2.02	2.04	2.95	Chromium
Aero Fancy	1.60	2.02	2.04	2.95	Chromium
Mickey Mouse	**1.60**	**2.02**	**2.04**	**2.95**	**Chromium**
Peggy Ingersoll	2.50	3.36	3.40	5.00	Chromium
CLOCKS					
Radiolarm	.83	1.04	1.05	1.50	Black
Mickey Mouse Alarm	**.83**	**1.04**	**1.05**	**1.50**	**Green**
Sunrise Alarm	1.07	1.36	1.38	2.00	Black or Ivory
Automobile Clock	.75	.94	.95	1.39	Chromium
ELTON LINE					10-K Rolled Gold Plate Top
Elton Wrist Plain	2.50	3.12	3.15	4.95	
Elton Wrist Fancy	2.50	3.12	3.15	4.95	Stainless Metal Back
PACEMAKER ASSORTMENT	9.44	11.90	12.02		

(2 Aero — **2 Mickey Mouse Wrist** —
2 Yankee—2 Ensign — Free Metal Display. Subject to withdrawal
without notice.)

TERMS—Freight will be allowed on shipments of 144 above watches; 144 above watches and clocks combined; 100 lbs. watches or clocks; or 100 lbs. watches and clocks combined.

SPECIAL NOTE – All orders are subject to acceptance by factory, and all quotations are subject to change without notice.

We do not ship less than 12 of any one watch model or 24 of any one clock model to our wholesale accounts.

THE INGERSOLL-WATERBURY COMPANY
31 Cherry Avenue, Waterbury, Conn.
111 North Canal Street, Chicago, Ill.

THE GEO. H. EBERHARD COMPANY
290 First Street, San Francisco. :-: *Pacific Coast Distributors*

(SEE REVERSE SIDE FOR WEIGHTS)

Ingersoll price list from July 1, 1935. Would you be willing to pay these prices today?

BIBLIOGRAPHY – Selected Reference Books

CARTOON COLLECTIBLES by Robert Heide & John Gilman, DOLPHIN-DOUBLEDAY
A CELEBRATION OF COMIC ART & MEMORABILIA by Robert Lesser, HAWTHORN
COLLECTIBLES: THE NOSTALGIA COLLECTOR'S BIBLE by Bert R. Sugar, QUICK FOX
COLLECTING TODAY FOR TOMORROW by David A. Herzog, ARCO
DISNEYANA by Cecil Munsey, HAWTHORN
JIM HARMON'S NOSTALGIA CATALOGUE by Jim Harmon, TARCHER/HAWTHORN

PUBLICATIONS – Newsletters, Newspapers and Magazines

ANTIQUE TOY WORLD
4419 Irving Park
Chicago, IL 60641

ANTIQUE TRADER
P. O. Box 1050
Dubuque, IA 52004

THE BUYER'S GUIDE
15800 Route 84 NE
Moline, IL 61244

COLLECTORS' SHOWCASE
P. O. Box 6929
San Diego, CA 92106

HOT-LINE
P.O. Box 6929
San Diego, CA 92106

HELP!

Your help is needed to make the next edition of *COLLECTING COMIC CHARACTER CLOCKS AND WATCHES* even bigger and better!

If you have any items not shown in the book, please contact me. I'd also like to obtain printed materials such as catalogues issued by manufacturers, distributors, wholesalers, jobbers and retailers, point-of-purchase displays, promotional literature, newspaper and magazine ads, store displays, price sheets, etc.

Also, if you worked for any of the comic character timepiece manufacturers during the 1930s, 1940s or 1950s, I'd like to hear from you.

Your contribution will be acknowledged in the next edition, plus you'll receive a free copy!

Write to me at:

HOWARD S. BRENNER
106 Woodgate Terrace
Rochester, NY 14625

4th Edition

Collecting Toys
A Collector's Identification and Value Guide
by Richard O'Brien

Richard O'Brien was assisted by the country's top toy experts in order to make this new 4th edition a truly magnificent guide for toy collectors. Each category has been increased greatly with more listings and illustrations. The toy soldier and battery-operated sections have been really beefed up. NOW INCLUDED . . . A COMPREHENSIVE SECTION ON FISHER-PRICE! The reader will also find histories on many of the manufacturers. 8½ x 11, 384 pages (8 in full color showing hundreds of pieces)

$14⁹⁵

American Premium Guide To
Electric Trains
Identifications and Values
by Richard O'Brien

This new 2nd edition again has it all: LIONEL, MARX, AMERICAN FLYER, IVES, BUDDY L, plus others. Each category has been added to with more listings and photos. This guide includes the engines, cars and accessories with descriptions, prices and photos. Richard O'Brien (author of "Collecting Toys") has had the aid of the top train collectors from across the country in making this the best guide on trains. 5¼ x 8¼, 8 pages in color, 328 pages.

$10⁹⁵

Other Collectors' Guides From Books Americana

POCKET KNIVES	$14.95	NORTH AMERICAN INDIAN POINTS	$ 7.95
OLD FISHING LURES	14.95	SCOUTING COLLECTIBLES	10.95
GOLF COLLECTIBLES	14.95	VINTAGE CLOTHING	10.95
BIRD DECOYS	14.95	OLDE CAMERAS	9.95
KITCHEN COLLECTIBLES	10.95	RECORD GUIDE	14.95
HUMMEL FIGURINES & PLATES	9.95	JUKEBOXES/SLOT MACHINES	10.95
OLD JEWELRY	10.95	FARM ANTIQUES	10.95
RHINESTONE JEWELRY	10.95	DEPRESSION-ERA GLASSWARE	10.95
AMERICAN INDIAN POTTERY	29.95	ART NOUVEAU	10.95
NORTH AMERICAN INDIAN ARTIFACTS	10.95	COLLECTOR PRINTS	14.95

P. O. Box 2326   Florence, Alabama 35630   (205) 757-9966